THE YOUNG ENTREPRENEUR'S GUIDE TO BUSINESS TERMS

THE YOUNG ENTREPRENEUR'S GUIDE TO BUSINESS TERMS

WRITTEN BY STEPHAN SCHIFFMAN

FRANKLIN WATTS
A DIVISION OF SCHOLASTIC INC.
New York · Toronto · London · Auckland · Sydney · Mexico City · New Delhi · Hong Kong
Danbury, Connecticut

Created in association with
Media Projects, Incorporated

Carter Smith, *Managing Editor*

Karen Covington, *Project Editor*

Amy Henderson, *Designer and Production Editor*

Oxygen Design: Sherry Williams
and Tilman Reitzle, *Cover Design*

Marilyn Flaig, *Indexer*

Franklin Watts Staff

Phil Friedman, *Publisher*

Kate Nunn, *Editor-in-Chief*

Veronica Haas, *Editor*

Marie O'Neill, *Art Director*

HOW TO USE THIS BOOK

Use this book to learn more about the world of the entrepreneur. It provides you with an A to Z overview of terms and concepts important to people who are interested in starting and running a business. Some of the most important definitions will feature full-page "close-up" articles to give you all the facts you need on particularly important topics. Within the text, you'll also find text boxes offering real-life examples that illustrate important ideas.

Along the way, you'll find profiles of young entrepreneurs who got their own businesses off the ground and who offer advice on the best ways to make sure your business succeeds.

Library of Congress Catologing-in-Publication Data

Schiffman, Stephan.
   The young entrepreneur's guide to business terms/Stephan Schiffman.
      p. cm. — (Watts reference)
   Summary: Includes definitions for an A to Z list of business terms that should be familiar to all potential entrepreneurs.
   Includes bibliographical reference and index.
   ISBN 0-531-14665-0
   I. Business—Dictionaries, Juvenile. [1. Business—Dictionaries.] 1. Title Guide to business terms. II. Title. III. Series.

HF1001.S34 2003
650'.03—dc21   2003043094

CONTENTS

What Is an Entrepreneur?

Henry Ford   Jeff Bezos

Almost a century ago, Henry Ford, founder of the Ford Motor Company, had a vision: a quality, affordable motorcar that the average American could use to drive to work, on leisure trips, or for any other purpose. The experts of the day told Ford it couldn't be done, that motorcars were—and would always be—a luxury item. Ford felt otherwise. He found a way to turn his vision into a reality and launched one of America's most successful industrial organizations. To do it, he had to launch a revolution of sorts. He changed the way automobiles—and a whole lot of other things—were manufactured in America. He made the Model T a household word.

Jeff Bezos, founder of amazon.com, had a vision, too: a giant on-line retailer that would change the way people shopped. He started his audacious new company out of a rented Bellevue, Washington, home in 1995—less than a decade ago. In 2001, the company posted its first profit—and silenced (for a while, at least) the many critics who insisted that the flashy on-line retailer would never make money. In the process, Bezos challenged—and altered—a lot of preconceptions about what a retailer "really" did. Amazon.com started out selling books, but now it sells nearly anything you can think of.

Both Ford and Bezos are special kinds of businesspeople. These kinds of business leaders are not just executives, not just decision makers, not just leaders—they're entrepreneurs. The most successful entrepreneurs have a vision of how they can help large groups of people. Sometimes that vision transforms an industry sector or helps to move the national or world economy to another level of development. Sometimes the results are a little less dramatic, of course, but the most successful (and happiest) entrepreneurs are driven by a vision.

While *The Young Entrepreneur's Guide to Business Terms* is primarily a practical dictionary of important terms and concepts, it's also more than that. Within these pages, you'll also find insight from young entrepreneurs who, like Henry Ford and Jeff Bezos, had a vision that they put into practice in starting their businesses. These young entrepreneurs share a number of qualities, but one of the most important is this one: When in doubt, entrepreneurs focus on their vision for attracting and helping customers!

What Is a Business Vision?

A business vision is something that:

- ▶ Helps a specific group of people (typically, your customers or target market).

- ▶ Keeps you busy, but feels more like play than work.

- ▶ Is closely connected to something you already know a great deal about or are eager to learn more about.

- ▶ Inspires you to take personal responsibility for the work necessary to turn the vision into a reality.

There are probably as many different visions as there are entrepreneurs. The point is, your vision should inspire you; if it doesn't, there's not much point in starting up a business in the first place.

Your vision might be to make it easier for people to keep their pets clean, or store their motorcycles more easily, or spend more time with their kids. For your first business, it's probably a good idea to start fairly small, and to identify a "niche" group of customers you can help as part of fulfilling your business's vision—the "why" of your business. Whatever that vision is, it should be something that automatically makes you feel better about spending time on it. As it happens, entrepreneurs like Ford and Bezos have to spend a great deal of time turning those visions into reality.

You can—and probably should—start with a vision, but eventually you have to turn the vision into a plan. One of the best ways to do that is to build up a formal business plan.

Kathryn Welsh   Eitan Feinberg   Anita Johnson-Jones

What Is a Business Plan?

Basically, a business plan is a written document that says what, exactly, your business is. It says what you want to accomplish (which is a pretty important thing to know) and it also serves as an in-depth résumé for your company—something you can show to investors, bankers, business advisors, and other important people.

In fact, most business plans are used to support a request to borrow money. The plan is designed to show potential investors or lenders why it makes economic sense to offer financial support for the company. The plan also lets investors know what kind of payback to expect in return and when.

Typically, the business plan includes:

- ◉ A summary of how you plan to succeed in your business and why it's a great idea.

- ◉ An analysis of your market—the people you plan to turn into customers.

- ◉ An in-depth look at your product or service.

- ◉ Specific information about the experience, background, and qualifications of all the important members of your team.

- ◉ Accurate financial information.

- ▶ Realistic financial projections that include all your relevant operating costs.

- ▶ If you're applying for a loan or trying to attract investors: An estimate of the total amount of money you think you'll need over a given period of time, and a summary of how you plan to spend that money.

There are a lot of different ways to put together a business plan, but some of the best advice can be found, via the World Wide Web, from the Small Business Administration. You can use their excellent business-plan development tool by visiting www.sba.gov/starting/indexbusplans.html—and you'll also find some of the SBA's advice on developing a business plan at the end of this book.

Even if you're not applying for a loan or trying to get money from investors, developing a detailed written business plan is an excellent idea. A good business plan will help you allocate your resources, deal with problems you didn't anticipate (and there will be quite a few), and make the right choices as your business grows. It will remind you—and your key team members and allies—about exactly why you started the business, what your most important goals are, and how, specifically, you've planned to turn the vision into a reality.

Josh Newman   Linda Torres-Winters

Speaking From Experience

I started my business—a sales training company—from scratch over two decades ago. Today it is one of the top ten sales training organizations in the country. I know, from personal experience, there are many ups and downs in the life of the successful entrepreneur. I hope you will share your questions, your challenges, and your successes with me, so that you can set out on this rewarding road with the right vision and right plan. Please e-mail me at: contactus@dei-sales.com

Good luck!

—Stephan Schiffman

The Random House Dictionary of the English Language defines an entrepreneur as someone who "organizes and manages any enterprise, especially a business, usually with considerable initiative and risk." That's a pretty good one-sentence definition, but it only goes so far. It really doesn't give a real-world sense of the energy, personality, or level of commitment necessary for success in this demanding line of work. To get a sense of whether or not you may be an entrepreneur, take a look at the following questions. Answer each one as honestly as you can; turn to page 120 to check your answers. The score you get will give you a more in-depth answer to the question:

Are You an Entrepreneur?

1 It's 8:40 P.M. on the night before you have to hand in a report, and you're about halfway done. You get a call from a friend reminding you that your favorite band in the whole world is hosting a television special in about twenty minutes. You'd completely forgotten about the show; you've been looking forward to this show all week. It will run for an hour and a half. Your friend wants you to call when it starts so the two of you can talk about the show. What do you do?

A) Do your best with the twenty minutes that you've got left, then turn on the tube and call your friend.

B) Apologize to your friend for not being able to talk on the phone; tape the show so you can watch it tomorrow night; spend the next hour and a half working on your report.

C) Stop working, chat with your friend until the show starts. You weren't enjoying working on the report that much anyway, and maybe the teacher will give you some extra time if you ask for it.

2 Of the following, which statement comes closest to describing how you really feel?

A) "It's tough out there. To get ahead in this world, you sometimes have to cut a few corners and tell a few little white lies."

B) "When I make a commitment, you can count on it. I don't say things if I don't really mean them."

C) "It's best to tell people the truth as often as you can…but let's be real. Sometimes, it's easier to say what people want to hear."

3 Your next-door neighbor is going on vacation for a week and a half. He's arranged to pay you to feed and walk his dog once a day. The neighbor made you promise to walk the dog at least once a day between noon and 1:00 in the afternoon. Which is likeliest to happen?

A) You'd need some help—and maybe a little nagging from your parents or someone else—to remember that you're supposed to walk the dog.

B) You might forget to walk the dog a few times over the course of the week and a half. But whose fault would that really be? The hour between noon and 1:00 in the afternoon is right in the middle of the day, and you've got other things to do, too.

C) One way or another, you would find a way to be sure that you remembered to feed and walk the dog each day between noon and 1:00.

4 Of the following, which statement comes closest to describing how you really feel?

A) "I like to have lots and lots of time to make important decisions."

B) "Most of the time, when I have to make up my mind about something that's really important, I'm afraid I'm going to make a big mistake. Sometimes that keeps me from making any decision at all."

C) "The choices I make are usually pretty good, and even if I'm short on time, I feel like I can trust my instincts."

5 Of the following, which of these statements comes closest to describing the way you really feel?

A) "I think about what reward I'm going to get from working, so even working at something that somebody else might think of as boring or difficult is usually easy for me. As a rule, I keep going until I finish whatever I'm doing."

B) "Putting in a lot of time on the job may be okay for some people, but after a while, I'm ready to kick back."

C) "I'm not really sure that working hard has much of a payoff."

6 Your dad asks you to help him set up a mailing he's doing. It looks like it could be a pretty complicated project; it involves using software neither of you has used before. If you do this, though, he'll buy you tickets for a concert you really want to see. Assume you're going to go ahead and do this job for your dad. Of the following, which is likely to be the best description of how you feel about the job?

A) "Show me what to do and I'll do it."

B) "Let's take a look at the software or the manual before we actually try to do anything; that way we can set up a plan for how we can make this mailing happen."

C) "Fire up the computer and let's get started; it will probably make sense as we go along."

7 Of the following responses, which comes closest to describing the way you really feel?

A) "When I have a good idea, it's usually not that hard for me to get other people to help out with it."

B) "If I make an effort, I may be able to convince somebody else to take action on something that I think is important."

C) "I prefer to let someone else take the lead when it comes to getting people fired up."

8 You did your best, but you turned some homework in late. What are you likeliest to say to the teacher when he asks you why?

A) "Hey, I did my best."

B) "It took longer to finish than I thought it would. I overscheduled myself."

C) "It's not my fault there's too much homework at this school."

accountant

A person who assembles and works with a company's financial information. An accountant may be a company employee, but is more often a person who works for another firm, and is hired to come in as an outsider to make sure that the client's financial records are in order. The accountant has many duties—including, for instance, preparing a business's **tax** returns. See also **certified public accountant**

accounting

The discipline that focuses on classifying, understanding, and explaining a company's financial records. Typically, an accountant assesses the work of a bookkeeper (see **bookkeeper**) and transforms those records into reports showing, among other things, a business's profit or **loss** for a given period of time. Accountants are responsible for reporting on a business's true financial condition and future prospects. Accountants must under-

Today, most accounting functions are computerized. Ledgers and calculators are rarely used for large-scale accounting tasks.

stand and analyze all the legal and financial factors that may affect a business's performance.

accounting systems

Formal strategies and methods for keeping track of financial information. Today, there are still some small businesses that maintain manual accounting systems (in which entries are recorded on preprinted paper forms); it is now much more common, however, for businesses of all sizes to use computer **software** programs to keep track of their financial information. Popular accounting software packages include Peachtree and Quicken.

acquisition

What happens when one company buys another. A company may purchase another company for **cash**, or by acquiring enough **shares** in the company to take control of the company. Sometimes, when a buying company wants the company badly enough, it will pay an even greater **price** per share to the shareholders than the shareholders could get by selling the **stock** to others. This means that the shareholders could make an even greater profit by selling shares to the acquiring company than they could if they sold the shares on the open market. There are several ways one company takes over another. As a group, these types of business dealings are called "mergers and acquisitions." See also **merger**

> Many stock market investors make a habit of looking for companies that they think are likely to become acquisition targets—that is, companies that some other company will soon try to take over by offering stockholders high prices for shares of its stock. This process usually drives up stock prices; if the investor buys before the acquisition campaign begins, he or she can make money by selling after the price of the stock rises.

advance

An amount of money paid before work on a project is done, as a **down payment**. Sometimes advances are paid for a specific purpose (such as covering travel **expenses**). Sometimes an advance is paid is to demonstrate to the person or business who receives the money that all the work will be paid for when it is finished. If you were to agree to create a simple **World Wide Web** site for a local business, you might charge $500—and ask for a $250 advance before beginning the work.

advertising

See page 15

affiliate program

A program allowing merchants to invite other merchants (usually in a related business) to advertise on a Web site by putting up banners (see **banner advertising**) or buttons meant to direct people to another Web site. For example, if you sold women's shoes on your Web site, you might have businesses that sell women's purses or dresses or other accessories advertise on your site. This form of advertising helps to pay for the cost of your Web site. An affiliate program is a little like renting a store in a shopping center—and then renting a counter in your store to someone who sells something related to your business. There are different kinds of affiliate programs; some are based on a flat monthly fee, while others are based on percentages of the income that arise from the referral.

agreement

A commitment to do something in return for something else. Agreements don't have to be in writing to be legally binding; some spoken agreements are "enforceable"—meaning a judge could decide to compel one of the parties to carry out his or her commitment. It is always better, though, for business agreements to be set in writing, because a written document is the best way to prove what both sides of the agreement actually committed to do. See also **contract**

The chairmen of Exxon and Mobil announce their agreement to merge their companies in 1998.

Traders at work on the floor of the American Stock Exchange (also known as the Amex) in New York City.

American Stock Exchange

The second largest trading exchange for **stocks** and **bonds** in the U.S. (The largest is the **New York Stock Exchange**.) It is located at 86 Trinity Place in downtown Manhattan. Generally speaking, stocks and stock **options** traded on this exchange—often called the Amex—are **shares** of small- to medium-sized companies. (Note: Companies that sell shares to the public are known as "publicly held" companies; a "small" publicly held company is still a major enterprise!)

appraisal

Steps you take to figure out how much a certain piece of property is worth. People often arrange for appraisals before selling something, or to evaluate **collateral** for an upcoming loan, or to determine how much **insurance** a person or business should purchase. An appraisal is usually made by a professional who is an expert in a certain field.

REAL LIFE: If you wanted to use your home as collateral for a business loan, the bank would arrange for an appraisal before it could approve the loan.

assets

Valuable things owned by a person or company. Assets can be **cash**, inventory, or personal property; assets must be wholly owned by the person or company. To determine whether they will loan money to a person or organization, banks try to determine the present value of the assets that can be used as **collateral** for the loan.

assign

The act of formally transferring ownership of something from one person or organization to another. People and companies may assign things like property, or rights to the repayment income from a loan, or rights granted by a previously signed **contract**. If you assign something to another person or entity, you're called the assignor; whoever receives the ownership is called the assignee.

audit

A detailed inspection of financial records by a special kind of expert **accountant** known as an auditor. Auditors may inspect financial records to make sure the person tracking financial information is doing the job correctly, maintaining accurate and complete records, and following accepted rules of **accounting**. An audit can be conducted by a person inside the organization (an "internal audit"), by an outsider (an "independent audit," usually conducted by a **CPA**), or by the **Internal Revenue Service** (a "tax audit"). Internal audits are generally meant to determine whether the company's policies and procedures are being followed, or to identify people who may be stealing money from the company (see **embezzler**). An independent audit can do the same job, and can also confirm that the company's **record keeping** is accurate for reports to stockholders. Tax audits conducted by the Internal Revenue Service are meant to find out whether the person or organization has been paying the correct tax.

advertising

A sponsored message designed to reach people and persuade them to take some kind of action. When we think of advertising, we usually think of a paid message sent over the radio, or on television, in a magazine or newspaper, or on the Internet, but advertising messages can be free of charge and can appear in any medium. Advertising messages are meant to induce people to do something—such as buy a certain brand of spaghetti or apply for a loan at a certain bank. Not all advertising is designed to get the viewer or listener to buy something; sometimes advertising is meant to send a message to inform the public about health or safety issues. (This type of advertising is known as "public service" advertising.)

Because most of the major advertising agencies once operated on Madison Avenue in New York City, the phrase "Madison Avenue" caught on as a way to describe the advertising industry as a whole.

Many people criticize the advertising industry for "manipulating" public opinion and for "creating" **demand** for products and services that add little value to the daily lives of consumers. Those in the advertising industry usually reply that their discipline is an important part of the modern **free enterprise system**, and that advertising and **promotion** cannot create demand for products and **services** that do not resonate with the public.

REAL LIFE: If you were to pay a local radio station to talk briefly about the grand opening of your new T-shirt store, you would be using advertising to promote your business.

Successful advertising campaigns can have a dramatic impact on a company's fortunes. In 2001, Dell Computer launched an advertising campaign featuring the character "Steven," an humorously appealing teen who touts the benefits of Dell's products. Ever since "Steven's" first appearance, Dell's revenues have increased dramatically.

balance sheet

A report meant to show the exact financial picture of a company on a certain date. A balance sheet includes the assets of a company (generally shown on the left side of the statement) and any claims against the company (generally shown on the right side). Included in the claims against the company, called the debit side, are the **liabilities**—such as loans and the owners' **equity** or **investment** in the company. The report is called a balance sheet because the left side and the right side totals must be equal, or "in balance."

bankruptcy

See page 18

banner advertising

A kind of advertising found only on the **World Wide Web**. When a person or company owns a Web page that attracts visitors, it can "rent out" advertising space on that page. In this way, owners of **Web sites** are able to generate advertising income for their company. See also **affiliate program**

ABC Company Balance Sheet

Assets

Current Assets:

Cash $130,000
Accounts Receivable $40,000
Less:
  Reserve for Bad Debts $5,000
  Merchandise Inventory $15,000
Total Current Assets $150,000

Fixed Assets:

Property and Equipment
  Furniture and Fixtures $40,000
  Improvements $15,000
  Office Equipment $155,000
Less:
  Accumulated Depreciation
  ....$125,000
Total Fixed Assets $85,000

Other Assets:

  Security Deposit (Rent) $2,500
Total Other Assets $2,500

Total Assets $240,000

Liabilities and Capital

Liabilities:

Accounts Payable $75,000
Sales Taxes Payable $5,000
Payroll Taxes Payable $5,000
Short-Term Bank Loan Payable
  ....$20,000
Total Liabilities $105,000

Capital:

Owner's Equity $50,000
Net Profit $85,000
Total Capital $135,500

**Total Liabilities
and Capital $240,000**

base

A means of measurement or standard amount. For instance, "base pay" is the amount of an employee's regular pay to which supplements are added, such as overtime or bonuses. "Base rent" refers to the number of dollars a landlord can count on receiving each month; added to that figure might be a percentage of the **sales** income made each month by the renter. (This type of rent is often applied to a store's rental in a mall, for example.) Other types of bases are nationally reported bases, such as the **Consumer Price Index** (CPI). This index is used as a way to measure whether prices of **goods** and **services** have gone up or down in comparison to prior years.

16

This illustration depicts the concept of a bear market. The graph shows the price of stocks dropping. As the value of stock diminishes, an investor looks concerned and grim.

bear market

A period of time when the average price of **stocks** falls for an extended period. A bear market is often a result of a belief that stock prices will continue to fall for some time to come. (The term may also be used in reference to **bonds**.) When bears attack, they do so by slashing in a downward motion; this is why the phrase came to be associated with downward market trends. When bulls attack, on the other hand, they thrust their horns upward. A bull market is, therefore, associated with an upward market trend. See also **bull market**

benchmark

The performance of a certain group of stocks over time; used to compare a company's stock performance with that of a larger group.

benchmark interest rate

The lowest interest rate **investors** will require for investing in a **security** not issued by the Treasury Department. It is tied to the most recently issued Treasury offerings.

benefits

Resources made available to employees by their employers. Typical benefits include health **insurance**, **pension plans**, 401(k) plans, etc.

beneficiary

A person or organization benefiting from a particular act of another. The beneficiary of a will or trust, or of money from an insurance claim, is the person designated to get the money or property at a certain point (for instance, the death of the person writing the will).

bankruptcy

The way that a **debtor** who cannot meet financial obligations resolves these obligations. When a person or a business cannot pay debts, United States federal law provides a legal way to avoid, put off, or pay less than the original debt amount. Bankruptcy can be "voluntary" (the person who owes money goes to court) or "involuntary" (the **creditor**(s) go to court in the hope of receiving their share of the debtor's **assets**). A person or organization declared bankrupt by a court faces limitations on future financial activities until the bankruptcy is "discharged." A type of bankruptcy filing known as "Chapter 11" (because of the portion of the federal bankruptcy law where it is found) allows a company to keep operating, protected from creditors, while reorganizing to repay money it owes. United States bankruptcy laws are more favorable to the debtor than in most other countries; this is because American laws have generally been written so as to encourage **investment** and risk-taking among individuals and businesses.

> When a business files for Chapter 11 bankruptcy protection, a judge will work with a court-appointed trustee, whose job is to figure out how much is owed and to whom.

REAL LIFE: During the dot-com boom, hundreds of thousands of people bought luxury items they couldn't afford and ran up high credit card bills. After the bust, many filed for bankruptcy to discharge their debt. Due to enormous increase in bankruptcy cases, Congress passed a law in 2001 making it more difficult for individuals and small businesses to seek bankruptcy protection.

Although there are numerous types of bids, a relatively new one is a bid placed over the Internet. Many Web sites hold online auctions. One company, the hugely successful eBay, is visited by thousands of people per day.

bid

A stated amount that a purchaser is willing to pay for a product or **service**. If the seller accepts the bid, the item(s) are sold to that bidder. If not, they may go to another person who has also put in a bid at a higher price, or offered more attractive terms.

bookkeeper

The person whose responsibility it is to enter all financial **transactions** into the company's **accounting** system, or "books."

bond

An obligation to pay; a **debt**. When you buy a bond, you make a loan to whoever is issuing the bond. Bonds come in a number of categories: government (federal, state, or municipal) or corporate. Many people prefer to buy municipal bonds, rather than corporate bonds or bonds from other entities, because municipal bonds are **tax**-free. (In other words, the person who gets the **interest** doesn't have to pay federal **income tax** on the interest income.) Interest on corporate bonds is taxable by both federal and state governments.

Corporate bonds are issued when a **corporation** needs to raise money. These bonds are rated according to the perceived ability of the business to pay its bondholders. Bonds issued by companies with high bond ratings are more expensive to buy, but are much safer for the **investor**.

A poster from World War I advertises government bonds.

bottom line

Net profit or **loss**. The bottom line is the company's (or a certain project's) financial position after all relevant **expenses** and taxes are paid.

The expression "What's the bottom line?" means, essentially, "Don't trouble me with details—what's the most important point?"

brand

A recognizable product or service name, typically one made popular because of **advertising** or word of mouth.

break-even point

The point at which a company's income equals its **expenses**. This is the point at which all the costs, both **fixed costs** and **variable costs**, can be paid out of income.

The term "break-even" is also used to refer to **stock** or **real estate** purchased at a certain time. With regard to stocks, this is the point when the current value of the stock is equal to the exact amount the stockholder originally paid for it. In real estate, it refers to the time when a building has enough occupancy income to pay all of the building's expenses, with nothing left over as profit.

broadcast advertising

Promotion by means of radio or television. Broadcast advertising is used to reach the broadest possible amount of people, since most people listen to radio or watch television. Other types of advertising include print (newspaper and magazine advertising) and **World Wide Web** advertising.

broker

Someone who brings together a buyer and a seller and receives a **commission** for doing so. Sometimes the commission is paid by the buyer, but it is more often paid by the seller. When a buyer has difficulty in finding a certain item he or she wants, the buyer will contact a broker. When the broker finds the desired item, the broker may receive a commission known as a finder's **fee**. There are many types of brokers, including stockbrokers, real estate brokers, and **commodities** brokers.

A man in a broadcasting studio sits in front of television screens and controls. He is in charge of, among other things, cutting from the network's program to the advertisements.

> "We are putting applications straight on the Internet— it's a very new industry."
>
> —Jayson Meyer

software solutions

POTENT QUOTES

HIGH POINTS OF RUNNING THE BUSINESS

"It's...something I really enjoy and always have. When I was a teenager, a teacher gave me $20 for helping out with one of the school's computers. That's when I started to think, Hey, this is something I enjoy doing."

LOW POINTS OF RUNNING THE BUSINESS:

"There are times in life and in business when you think about giving up...the key to everything...is staying focused and putting hard work and effort into it."

SAGE ADVICE:

"Maintain your integrity, find something that you really enjoy doing, and never, ever give up."

Working with his older brother, Martin Meyer, Jayson co-founded Meyer Technologies in 1996. At that time, Jayson was only thirteen years old! These days Meyer Technologies is working on creating online applications and databases. According to Jayson, it won't be long before everyone will get rid of CD-Roms and floppy disks and go online to get their necessary applications. Many of the major computer software companies, including Microsoft, are working toward the same goal as well. Rather than fear his major competition, Jayson hopes that Microsoft's new Web-based software plan called .Net will actually help build more interest in the software project he is currently working on.

Today, Meyer Technologies has launched a successful subsidiary, called Worksmart MD, which develops software resources that help medical offices ensure that they are in compliance with an important federal law, the Health Insurance Portability and Accountability Act, as well as help to automate doctor's offices and do electronic billing. Somehow, in the midst of running a high-tech company, Jayson manages to find the time to go out and speak to young people. He has also given several motivational speeches in southern Florida, as well as held question and answer sessions with students.

To find out more: Log on to www.worksmartmd.com

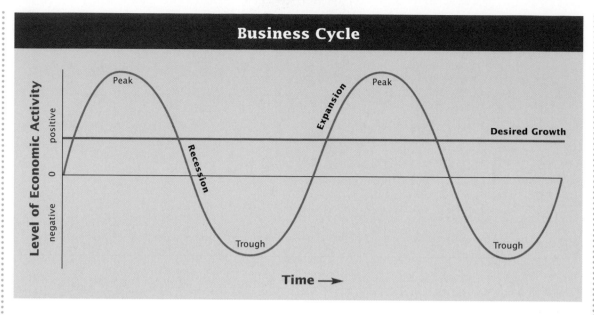

Business Cycle

Level of Economic Activity

positive / 0 / negative

Peak

Recession

Expansion

Peak

Desired Growth

Trough

Trough

Time →

bull market

A period of time when the price of stocks tends to go up. Bull markets are often the result of a belief that prices will continue to rise over a prolonged period. When used to describe bonds, the phrase usually refers to a lowering of **interest rates**. See also **bear market**

bulletin board

A place where people post messages. The phrase originally referred to actual cork boards; today, it also describes computerized communications systems that allow users with shared interests to post electronic notices to a group.

burn rate

The speed at which a new company goes through money before generating income above its **expenses**. When a new company starts up, it has to raise money to get organized, advertise, purchase necessities, and so on. Many companies raise money known as **venture capital**, provided by **investors**; this money is intended to pay for the costs of starting up a new business. At some time, it is expected that the company will begin to turn a profit. The rate at which the new company spends money before spending all of its venture capital (or burning out), is known as the burn rate. This figure is determined by dividing the amount of venture capital by the estimated period of time it will take to use those funds up.

business cycle

The recurrent cycle of **recession** and expansion in an economy. The high points of the expansion phase of the cycle are known as "peaks;" the low points of the recession phase of the cycle are known as "troughs."

business plan

A document outlining a company's situation and business strategy. Often, the business plan is meant to show what a person or group has to offer in the way of skill, what the anticipated markets will be, and how much money will have to be borrowed to go forward. Banks and other lenders typically require that they see a business plan before they move forward and lend money to a new venture.

call

An **option** on a **stock**, to be bought and paid for in the future. The call specifies the number of **shares**, the **price** that the buyer wishes to pay, and the date on which the buyer wishes to buy. The buyer pays for the option, or right, to buy at that price on that date; if the buyer decides not to purchase at that time, the buyer does not have to buy, but loses the price of the call.

"Call" also refers to a lender's right to decide to demand payment of a loan. Calling a loan makes the entire amount of the loan due and payable immediately.

> Calling a loan usually occurs when the borrower fails to meet some or all of the terms of the loan—for example, failing to make a payment on the date it is due.

call center

Facility at which company representatives connect with prospects and/or customers by phone to address **sales** issues, **service** issues, or both. Large mail order, catalog, or **Internet** sales are made by calling an order in to a call center. Call centers are also used to reach out to prospective customers. Call centers may be located far from the central business that owns them; many companies operate call centers, and pay for operators or salespeople who take or make calls on behalf of other companies.

A woman makes phone calls at a call center.

capital

Money invested in a company. See also **working capital**

capital gain

The amount of money a person gets when he/she sells a capital **asset**. Capital assets are assets that are held for long periods of time and not sold as a matter of course in operating a business; a house, a factory, a piece of machinery, or a commercial building might be considered a capital asset.

A capital asset is a long-term asset that you buy and then sell. A capital gain, which is different from **salary** income or other regular income, is the money you get as a result.

capital gains tax

A federal tax, generally lower than the **rate** of taxation for regular **income tax**. A company or individual pays tax on the profit realized when selling a capital asset.

REAL LIFE: If you sell a commercial building which you bought x number of years ago, and realize a profit from the sale, the amount of your profit is taxed as a capital gain.

cash

Generally paper currency and coins. The word may also include checks, bank accounts (cash on hand), and any **transactions** made in cash. The word "cash" is sometimes used even more broadly to distinguish between instruments that can quickly be cashed (such as a check) and **securities**.

> "To cash" means to convert instruments other than cash—such as a check—into currency.

cash and equivalents

Includes currency and similar instruments, such as travelers' checks or bank certified checks. The phrase may also include invested money that can easily be turned into cash (such as money market funds).

cash dividend

A payment made to the stockholders of a **corporation** from current or accumulated profits. A cash dividend is distinguished from a stock dividend, which is distributed to shareholders instead of cash, and which gives the shareholder a greater percentage in the company.

cash flow

All the money coming into and going out of a business. The cash income of a business includes money received when buyers pay the business for **goods** or **services** received, and from other sources, such as money received from loans. **Investors** watch a corporation to make sure it has sufficient cash flow to meet its **expenses**, including **dividends** to investors. Cash flow is not the same as profit.

> Cash flow totals do not take into account how much of the money received is taxable. Similarly, they do not take into account how much of the money will be used to pay bills, or whether there is any depreciation on equipment purchased.

caveat emptor

An ancient Latin term for a business warning that literally means "Let the buyer beware." The phase describes a legal principle that failure to live up to a bargain is not the seller's problem... *except* where the failure can be shown to violate a **contract**.

Today, many laws protect **consumers** from faulty acts of manufacturers. Recently, a general movement toward safeguarding consumers' rights has led to the development of a new doctrine, *caveat venditor* (let the seller beware), which places more responsibility on those selling a product or **service**.

central bank

A bank where all the reserves of other banks are held. The central bank issues a country's currency, stabilizes prices, provides economic growth, and regulates **interest rates**. The **Federal Reserve System** is the central bank of the United States.

A certified public accountant hard at work.

certified public accountant (CPA)

An accountant who by education, training, and licensing is qualified to perform **accounting** and auditing, and to prepare **income tax** returns for individuals and companies. A CPA has to have a special college education and pass difficult tests in order to be certified.

chain store

Generally a **retail** store belonging to a large group of similar stores and usually known by the same name (such as Wal-Mart or K-Mart). Such stores are usually managed by a central parent organization.

Some chain stores, like Staples, sell only products related to a specific industry.

checking account

A bank account, usually offered by a **commercial bank**, that allows people or organizations to withdraw funds or pay money to others by writing checks. Little or no **interest** is paid on a checking account, so most businesses do not leave large sums of money in their checking accounts. See also **savings account**

"From what we get, we can make a living; what we give, however, makes a life."

—Arthur Ashe, tennis player

Chicago Mercantile Exchange

A major international **exchange**, based in Chicago, Illinois, where one can buy **options** and future **investments** in **stock** indexes, **interest rates**, **commodities** such as foodstuffs, minerals, and foreign currencies. These types of investments are often considered "high-risk," and are usually engaged in by specialists.

churning

The practice of trading more often than is necessary in order to increase commissions.

REAL LIFE: When a **broker** advises you to buy and sell investments more often than is necessary for your account, and you follow that advice, you are a victim of churning. The broker is more interested in earning commissions than in the health or safety of your investments.

closing

In **real estate**, the point when an **agreement** is made final by the transfer of the **deed** and by the payment in full of the purchase **price**, either by a **cash** payment or the arrangement of a **mortgage**, and by taking care of all other issues connected with the sale.

The term can also be used to describe the finalization of a business loan, or the closing of the books at the end of the year in **accounting** practice. Salespeople use the term to describe the process of reaching a formal business agreement with a prospect; this kind of closing is usually accompanied by the signing of a contract or the completion of some other formal indication of commitment.

closing costs

Any of a variety of **fees** and **expenses** included in the cost of concluding a real estate sale. These can involve title insurance, recording of the deed, **appraisal** fees, attorneys' fees and **commissions**, and origination fees (sometimes called "points") on the mortgage.

coinsurance

The predetermined amount that an insurance company will not pay when there is damage to property (from fire, for instance, or from some other kind of **loss** to property), leaving the

A man uses a computer database to select potential customers to cold call.

owner to cover the difference. The owner may have to pay a percentage of the loss because of his or her failure to maintain the amount of insurance required to cover the full value of the property.

REAL LIFE: If you are required to cover a piece property up to 100 percent of its value, and you cover it up to only 80 percent, the insurance company will pay only 80 percent of the claim, no matter how small the claim; you, the owner, will have to pay 20 percent of the remaining costs. The 20 percent in this example is known as coinsurance.

cold call

A **prospecting** phone call made to potential customers of a particular product or **service** whom you don't yet know. The phrase is also used to refer to a personal visit to someone who has not yet heard of your product or service, and who is not expecting an in-person visit. Salespeople are often intimidated by the task of making cold calls, but prospecting by phone is one of the most important selling skills.

> **Merriam-Webster's dictionary cites 1966 for the first use of the phrase "cold call" to mean a telephone sales call made with no prior contact.**

collateral

An item of value (such as a house, **stock** in a company, a car, or jewelry) the **title** to which is left with a potential lender as **security** for a loan. If you fail to repay the loan, the lender can repossess your collateral. Sometimes actual items of personal property (such as jewelry) are left with the lender as collateral.

> "Love everybody who logs onto your site, and answer every e-mail."
>
> —Karen Tom

e-zine entrepreneur

Planet Kiki is a fun-filled virtual universe of everything a teenaged gal needs to know to get by in this world. The site's many young fans think of it as a virtual gathering place for those moments when life can be…shall we say…challenging.

The site's mastermind is Karen Tom, who has built, with designer Matt Frost, a unique Web site whose mission is to create an empowering and fun community for girls to share thoughts, dreams, feelings, and anything else they want to. It is the "planet's" inhabitants that make Planet Kiki so distinctive. The site includes poetry, art, essays, beauty tips, movie and book reviews, and just about anything else of interest to the community it serves. The site

has inspired a poetry anthology: *ANGST! Teen Verses from the Edge*; it was a finalist for the honor of Best Book for Young Adults from the National Library Association in 2002, and won a Quick Pick for Reluctant Readers Award from the same organization.

What motivated Karen to start Planet Kiki? "It seemed like a fun idea, and I love having interaction with the girls. That was really the guiding idea for the whole site."

To find out more: Log on to www.planetkiki.com

POTENT QUOTES

HIGH POINTS OF RUNNING THE BUSINESS:

"Being named the best online e-zine by TWIST magazine."

LOW POINTS OF RUNNING THE BUSINESS:

"Keeping up with all the correspondence. Fortunately, Kiki helps."

SAGE ADVICE:

"Love everybody who logs onto your site, and answer every e-mail. It works for us: Today, Planet Kiki's inhabitants are stationed throughout the U.S., Europe, Asia, Australia, and South America—reaching places like Croatia, United Arab Emirates, and Nicaragua!"

A customer makes a transaction with a teller at a commercial bank.

collection float

The time between the deposit of funds in an account and the time when the funds are available to depositors. Many banks and credit **unions** delay the availability of funds to their customers. Supposedly, this is in order to make sure that the banks and credit unions will actually receive funds from the deposited check. However, the process also allows banks to improve their own **cash** position, because they earn interest on deposits that have been verified, but have not yet been made available to customers. Current U.S. law requires that banks make deposits on local checks available within two days, and deposits on out-of-state checks available within five days.

collection agency

A person or organization collecting **debt** on behalf of others. Businesses sometimes employ agencies to collect debts that would otherwise not result in revenue for the **creditor**. Attorneys sometimes act as collection agents.

commercial bank

A business bank providing many different kinds of **services** to depositors and customers. In most cases, money deposited with a commercial bank is insured by the federal government. See also **Federal Deposit Insurance Corporation (FDIC)**

commercial paper

Short-term **financing** notes, which usually have to be paid in from 2 to 270 days. The paper is generally issued by banks, **corporations**, and other borrowers, through specialized **brokers**, and made available to **investors** who are actually the lenders of the money. These short-term loans are usually unsecured.

commission

A **fee** earned by an employee or agent for services performed. Commissions may be paid instead of, or in addition to, a **salary** (in the case of an employee); they may also be the fee paid to an outside individual or company for services (such as bringing a potential buyer and seller together).

> For employees, commissions can be used as incentives to encourage certain workplace activities. Salespeople who receive a commission for each sale are encouraged to increase their incomes by increasing the number of sales they complete.

commodity

A raw product derived from animal, vegetable, or mineral matter and traded on the open **market**. People sometimes refer to any popular and broadly distributed product or service as a commodity, but the term actually refers to some "fixed physical substance" bought and sold by investors for profit. Examples include pork

Wheat is a commodity that is bought and sold in the marketplace.

bellies, wheat, oil, and precious metals. These items are bought and sold on an **exchange**, just like stocks and bonds. See also **futures**

common stock

A **share** of ownership in a **corporation**. Shares of public corporations can be bought and sold on one of the stock exchanges on which the shares are listed. Shares in private companies called "closely held corporations" are generally not traded on the open **market**; they are usually held by original **investors** or the families of the original investors. Common stock holders elect the board of directors that runs the company. See also **preferred stock**

community relations

A category of business activity devoted to enhancing the image and position of an organization within a given community. Community relations is often identified as "giving something back" to a specific geographical, social, or demographic group in a way that improves the standing of the organization and helps the community in question. Many large companies go out of their way to develop positive relationships with local businesses, charities, and other members of the communities. These companies may have departments and staff whose primary job is to work with the community to aid specific causes and, not coincidentally, to enjoy **public relations** benefits in the form of positive media coverage for the company. Directors of community affairs often serve on charitable boards or committees dedicated to the betterment of the community; they may act as a liaison, or contact person, between the company and a certain community.

competition

Rivalry within the same or different **markets** for the same **customers**. Two companies that appeal to the same kinds of people or organizations to buy similar products or **services** are regarded as competitors. Competition enriches the economy as a whole and encourages cre-

Two young shoppers compare different brands of blue jeans.

A agreement reached through compromise is symbolized by a handshake.

ativity and closeness to the **customer**. In most cases, the company that does the best job of **marketing** itself and delivering both quality and value to customers will establish an advantage over the competition; there are, however, many factors that can tip the balance toward one competitor rather than another.

> Of the healthy economic effects of competition, industrialist Andrew Carnegie once wrote: "While the law [of competition] may sometimes be hard for the individual . . . it insures the survival of the fittest in every department."

complaint resolution

The processes companies put in place to deal with problems that **customers** have with products or **services** purchased from the company. Companies will sometimes give a **refund** to an dissatisfied customer, process a new order at a cheaper **price**, or take other steps to make the customer feel that the company will go out of its way to make the customer happy again. The goal of complaint resolution policies and procedures is simple: to find a way to maintain the relationship with the customer over the long term.

compromise

A situation where two or more people or businesses are involved in a dispute, negotiation, or similar discussion, and each gives up a part of their demand in order to conclude the deal.

conglomerate

A number of companies operating under the same corporate ownership. Conglomerates are usually in a variety of businesses. The thinking behind conglomerates is that a large conglomerate can provide better **management** and more resources, financial and otherwise, than small independent companies.

consumer

A person who purchases **goods** and services at the **retail** level.

Consumer Price Index (CPI)

Statistical measure published by the U.S. government that measures the amount of change in prices paid by urban consumers for a variety of goods. The Consumer Price Index, or CPI, monitors the cost of such items as food, housing, and transportation. It is often used to calculate the relative costs of items in different years. The Consumer Price Index began tracking price changes in 1913.

consumption

The use of **goods** to satisfy desires or to create some new product or **service**.

contract

A legally binding agreement or **exchange** of promises between two or more individuals. A contract can be spelled out on paper or in an **e-mail** exchange. See also **agreement**

contractor

An individual or company performing work for another as a contract worker, rather than as an employee. Contractors do not have **income taxes** withheld from their pay; they are required to report income to the government and then pay taxes on money received. As a general rule, they work from project to project and perform jobs in return for money. A good example of a group that often work as contractors are lawyers. Most lawyers charge their clients, but are not employed by them.

copyright

The exclusive legal right to copy, **market**, and sell some kind of **intellectual property** (such as a novel, a painting, a photograph, or a musical composition). A copyright prohibits any other person from exploiting the copyrighted material without the express permission of the copyright holder.

corporation

A formally registered business organization operating, under the law, as an individual. A corporation limits the **liability** of the owners of the corporation for the **debts** or other acts of the corporation.

Some of the leading figures in a corporation meet to discuss the company.

customer

Someone who purchases a product or **service**. The "customer base" is the total number of customers serviced by a given company. The part of an organization committed to interacting with customers and helping them resolve questions or issues is known as Customer Service.

Today, many customer-service issues are addressed through automated telephone lines or by means of the **Internet**. Some customers perceive the trend toward customer service that takes place without direct

> One popular customer service philosophy is "The customer is always right." This phrase means that a staff, particularly at retail organizations, must always find a way to satisfy the business's customers. H. Gordon Selfridge coined the phrase in the 19th century; Selfridge ran a successful chain of retail outlets.

interaction with live staff as frustrating or dissatisfying, but the trend toward handling customer-service issues with technology, rather than trained staff members, is likely to continue because it represents a significant cost savings to large organizations.

cost per thousand (CPM)

A common unit of **price** measure. The letter "M" is the Roman numeral for one thousand. The prices of items that are not usually purchased individually, but rather in much larger quantities, are sometimes quoted in "per thousand" costs.

covenant

An **agreement** or promise to do, or not to do, a certain thing. A covenant is often included in a formal contract with the words, "I covenant that I will…" (An example of such a covenant might be "I covenant that I will not compete in business with the ABC Company once it purchases my business.") Sometimes a covenant is included in a **deed** to **real estate**; the covenant gives the holder of the deed certain rights or imposes certain restrictions.

credit

A way to purchase **goods** or **services** by promising to pay for them in the future. An example might be a car bought on credit. Credit may also be the amount of money a business or individual is able to borrow at any given point in time. This is often called available credit. A credit card is a card used to make a purchase with funds forwarded, at **interest**, from a lending agency (such as American Express). A borrower's capacity to repay is often described in terms of "good" credit, or "bad" credit,

depending on the recent record of interactions with creditors. The word "credit" may also refer to goods or services due to a customer that are offered in place of a **cash** refund.

> The word "credit" is related the Latin word "credo," which means "I believe." Someone who extends credit to you believes that you will pay the money back in the future.

creditor

A person or company to whom a person or business owes money. A creditor might be someone who has loaned the business money, or it might be a **supplier** of **merchandise** or services whose bill has not yet been paid.

A businessman inserts a CRM software CD-Rom into his computer.

CRM software

Computer software designed to help organizations keep track of and effectively service their **customers**. CRM stands for Customer Relationship Management. Many CRM software packages are closely customized to match the industry or the individual company in which they are used.

customer

See page 33

database

A sortable collection of information that can be arranged, analyzed, and displayed with a computer system. Information collected over time can be extremely valuable to a company. Database **software** allows companies to collect the names, addresses, telephone numbers, and purchase history of **customers**—and then arrange that information by zip code to decide which customers should hear about a new product offering. (The use of a database to target groups with certain **demographic** qualities is part of a discipline known as "database marketing.") It is a wise idea for companies to frequently update their database to keep up with current clients.

day trader

Someone who trades **stocks** by watching the **market** constantly and buying and selling frequently—within a single day. This type of trader is typically looking for profitable deals that can be rechanneled instantly into a new trade; even a small profit will suffice.

debt

Money borrowed from a person or institution. Borrowing money is often essential for a company's success because it creates the means for a company's ability to grow.

debtor

Someone who borrows money.

deduction

The act of taking away, subtracting, or withholding something. A deduction typically refers to an amount of money.

deed

A signed and, typically, sealed document that conveys rights of ownership or other information about a legal transfer of some kind.

A day trader sits at his desk, ready to do business by buying and selling stock via an Internet Web site.

When a piece of real property, for instance, is sold or transferred, a new deed must by written that gives all the rights of ownership to the new owner. Deeds are used to transfer rights from the past owner, called the "grantor," to the new owner, called the "grantee."

default

Failure of a person or institution who owes money to make a payment when the **debt** becomes due. The word may also refer to the most common settings on a computer or a piece of **software**.

delivery

The transfer of **goods** or legal ownership to property. The process may involve physical transfer or some kind of symbolic transfer, such as giving a **deed** to a new owner.

demand

The desire of **customers** to have a certain product or **service**, combined with the ability to pay. Demand must contain the willingness to pay, at the stated price, for the desired item, not just the desire for it.

demographics

A way of defining a segment of the population, or a portion of a prospective customer base, by using statistics. Groups can be defined by age, sex, income, family size, occupation, or other factors. These factors can define a segment of the population that marketers target. Demographic questions are usually considered early in

This group of young adults represents a certain portion of the general population. They are a demographic defined by age.

> "If you are not failing now and again, it's a sign you're playing it safe."
>
> — Woody Allen, filmmaker

the development of a product, and may determine the kind of **advertising**, packaging, and terms used in this type of **marketing**.

REAL LIFE: If you were to promote a new brand of facial soap intended to appeal to women between the ages of 18 and 24, with household incomes over $100,000, you would be focusing your marketing efforts based on certain demographics.

depreciation

An allowance for the "using up" of a piece of equipment, or other property used to produce income. The government allows business owners of this kind of property a **tax** advantage to compensate for the aging of equipment and the shortening of its time of usefulness. Because high-tech equipment changes at such a rapid rate, the **Internal Revenue Service** allows faster rates of depreciation for computers and other high-tech products than they do for other business-related equipment. The word also refers to the process by which anything loses value or becomes obsolete over time.

direct mail

A **marketing** strategy that uses mail to deliver promotional pieces directly to **consumers**. Direct mail, unlike some other forms of **advertising**, can be targeted to a very specific audience. Advertisers who mail such pieces in a large amount can obtain a bulk mailing permit for a cheaper rate than first class mail.

discount

Selling at a **price** lower than the standard or market price. The word may also refer to a reduction in the amount of money owed offered as an incentive for early payment or payment in some specified manner.

discussion group

A group of persons interested in a particular topic who share insights and opinions about that topic. Today, many discussion groups take place through **e-mail** messages and electronic **bulletin boards**.

Many companies transport their products from the manufacturer to the retailer and into the hands of the potential customers by truck.

distribution channel

A group of interdependent entities that involve themselves in the process of getting **goods** and **services** to **end users**. Choosing a distribution channel is a critical **management** decision with major implications for a company's overall marketing strategy.

> "I (have spreadsheets) that show my total revenue from each month, my total profits, and my total percentage of return on investment."

— Kevin Hanks

recycled bicycles

This Wilbraham, Massachusetts, teen recently won the first MassMutual Entrepreneurial Scholar Award, and was singled out as one of 17 students (out of a possible 29,000) for honors from the National Foundation for Teaching Entrepreneurship. He was also named a Young Entrepreneur of the Year. So what's all the fuss about?

Kevin Hanks is the proud proprietor of Mass-Bike, a business that sells reconditioned, used bicycles. Kevin started the company when a neighbor gave him several old bikes in desperate need of major repair. Kevin fixed all the bikes, then he placed a "For Sale" sign on his lawn and sold all of them for about $35 to $40 each. Inspired by his initial success, Kevin then took out an ad for his repaired bikes in a local free paper. As his business and reputation grew, so did the demand for bikes. Finally, Kevin made the move to the high-tech marketing plan that won him all those entrepreneur accolades. He built an on-line auction site that attracts buyers for his bikes from all over the United States.

To find out more: Visit www.mass-bike.net

POTENT QUOTES

HIGH POINTS OF RUNNING THE BUSINESS:
Don't let the customer down "I know I'm going to come through with the product, but (customers) don't. It's my job to prove it."

LOW POINTS OF RUNNING THE BUSINESS:
Keeping enough bikes in stock! "If I had the inventory...I could do $1200 to $1300 a week in revenue and gross $875–$900."

SAGE ADVICE:
Keep good records "I have a notebook strictly designated for Internet business, and I have the auction papers on hand for each bike."

diversification

The act of adding diversity or variety to minimize risk by balancing something (such as a stock **portfolio** or a business's operations) across more than one category.

dividend

Payments taken from the profits of a **corporation** and paid to common and preferred shareholders. A **stock** worth $20 per **share** with an annual dividend of $1 yields the **investor** 5 percent. Dividends paid to individual shareholders are taxable as ordinary income. Since dividends are part of the corporation's income, they are subject to corporate taxation.

Dow Jones Industrial Average (DJIA)

A figure averaging the values of 30 major publicly held American corporations. The DJIA provides an indicator of how all of these stocks—and, by extension, the stock **market** as a whole—perform each day. This average is followed closely by most investors and analysts. Companies like Exxon, IBM, Goodyear, and General Motors are included in the DJIA, which occasionally changes the 30 companies whose performance it monitors. Despite criticism from analysts that the "Dow" features too few companies to be an accurate representation of the market as a whole, or that weaker-priced stocks on the index can sometimes produce disproportionate swings in the average, the DJIA remains one of the most widely watched and influential indexes in the world. See also **NASDAQ**

> **The Dow Jones Industrial Average was created in the late 19th century by Charles Dow, one of the founders of the Dow Jones Company and the first editor of the *Wall Street Journal*.**

down payment

The portion of an amount due that is paid in **cash** when one buys property by means of a loan with a long-term payout (such as a car loan or a piece of **real estate**).

A man uses an Automated Teller Machine (ATM) to draw money from an account.

draw

1. The act of taking money out of a bank account or other fund of one's own. For example, writing a check or a draft to deduct money from a **checking** or **savings account** is considered a draw.

2. To receive a predictable amount of money on a regular basis against future **commissions**. When the commission **sales** materialize, the amount of the draw is then deducted from the commission payments.

3. To receive money in advance of a payment or work for a particular project.

earnest money

An amount of money offered to a seller, generally to secure a **contract**, and applied to the purchase **price**. Earnest money shows that the buyer really wants to buy, and is acting in "good faith." The practice is generally used in **real estate transactions**.

earnings

The amount left to distribute after all **expenses** of the corporation are paid. In a publicly held company, earnings are the portion of income from which a public company can pay **dividends** to its shareholders. The amount before **taxes** are paid is called pre-tax earnings.

Several hundred dollars represent earnings.

earnings per share

In a publicly held company, the total amount of profit, divided by the total amount of outstanding shares of the company's **stock**.

e-commerce

The portion of the **economy** that involves buying and selling products and **services** over the **Internet**. Today, you can buy almost anything **online**. You can find the best deal for a particular item (say, an album by your favorite singer) by searching the Internet; you can decide to buy it or compare it with similar products; and you can pay for it and arrange shipping, all by using your computer. Both individuals and companies use the Internet to buy **goods** and services.

economics

The study of the interaction between producers, **consumers**, and workers in a given society.

economy

The financial health, stability, and well-being of a particular society.

electronic funds transfer system

YOUR ACCOUNTS
Checking
Savings
Money Market
Credit Cards
Business
Personal

BANK ONLINE

A way for a bank or other financial institution to make payments electronically. These systems are dependent on a series of debits and **credits** by member institutions. For example, if a member bank of the system makes a million dollars in payments, that payment is withdrawn electronically from the member's account. The member also deducts these payments from its individual account holders. When other member banks have paid an amount into the account of the first member bank, the total is credited back to that bank's account. These debits and credits flow back and forth, without any currency changing hands.

Many individuals use this system of payments **online** by authorizing certain organizations to deduct the amount of their bills, automatically, from their bank account.

e-mail

Electronic messages that travel between computers. E-mail messages have become an important part of business and social life; they can include attachments such as **word processing** documents, music files, or images. The message lands in the electronic "mailbox" of the other party until it is retrieved by the person to whom it is addressed.

E-mail is a convenient, inexpensive way to keep in touch with key people; it is also used to maintain **customer** relationships and sell products. Use of e-mail as a mass **marketing** tool has been controversial. See also **spam**

embezzler

A person who improperly takes the money of a company for himself or herself. Embezzlement is a criminal act.

A mother and daughter shop for clothes. They are the end users who ultimately purchase the company's product.

end user

The person or company for whom a product is intended, after it goes through all the various stages of its development, marketing, and sale.

endowment funds

Funds designed to deliver **interest** payments over time for a charitable institution. These funds are substantial enough to generate income for use by the institution.

The principal of an endowment fund is not intended to be used; its sole purpose is to generate interest payments.

> "Luck is a matter of preparation meeting opportunity."
>
> —Oprah Winfrey, media mogul

equity

A portion of ownership in a piece of property or business. The word may also refer to a company's amount of investment **capital** and retained **earnings**.

Finally, equity can mean fairness and the capacity to do the right thing. In legal circles, "equitable relief" is a kind of redress for past harm that cannot be reversed by money, but requires some kind of specific action.

exchange

1. To give one thing for another of equal value. **Retail** stores often prefer to exchange a product rather than accept a return for **cash**.
2. A place, such as the **New York Stock Exchange**, where things like **securities** or **commodities** are traded.

expense

A cost of doing business or maintaining property for a business purpose. Basically, expenses are money used to buy materials or **services** to generate income for a business. Examples of such costs may include **advertising**, supplies, or wages.

expiration date

The last day specified by an **agreement**, **contract**, or **option**.

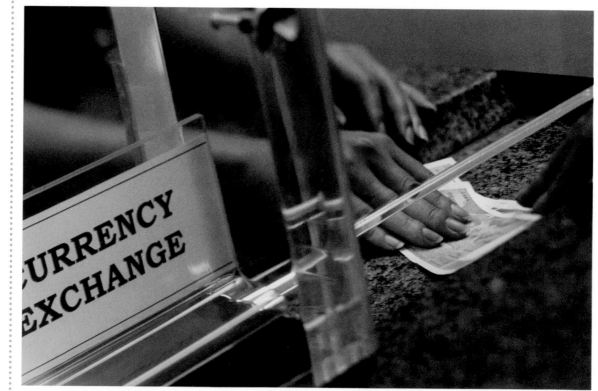

At a currency exchange money from one country is exchanged for money from another.

face value

The value imprinted on a financial instrument (such as a check, a **share** of **stock**, or a **bond**). The amount of face value on a check is the real value, but on a **security** the face value can differ from the **market** value (the amount someone is willing to pay for it).

fair market value

As a general rule, this is the **price** that would be agreed upon between a willing and knowledgeable buyer and a willing and knowledgeable seller in normal circumstances.

> If you were interested in learning the fair market value of a house in a particular neighborhood, you would want to know the prices of other, similar houses in the same neighborhood that had been sold over a given period of time. From those numbers, you could make an estimate of the fair market value of the house.

fair price

The price that a willing buyer will purchase for and willing seller will sell for. See also **fair market value**

Federal Deposit Insurance Corporation (FDIC)

An independent federal agency established in 1933 that insures deposits for up to $100,000 per account in member **commercial banks**,

While a vault safeguards money in a commercial bank, the FDIC protects it further.

which pay for the insurance. The FDIC provides important protection to **consumers**. If a member bank ever found that it didn't have enough money to operate, and were closed down, the FDIC would make sure that the depositors got their money back (or at least up to $100,000 of it). The FDIC also makes rules

43

Federal Reserve System

Sometimes known simply as the Fed, it is the United States' **central bank**. Its main function is to regulate the U.S. banking and monetary system. Founded in 1913 by an act of Congress under President Woodrow Wilson, it consists of 12 member regional banks and 25 branches of national and state banks. In each region the national banks are stockholders of the Federal Reserve Bank in their region.

In addition to establishing the nation's monetary policy, regulating banking institutions, maintaining stability in the financial system, and providing financial services, the Federal Reserve System supervises the printing of money and acts as a clearinghouse by transferring funds through the banking system.

The Federal Reserve System's influence has grown over the years. Its primary job is to affect money and **credit** conditions in the United States in a way that supports low inflation and high employment. The Fed controls the federal funds **rate**, which in turn usually affects other rates, such as bank lending rates and **mortgage interest rates**.

The **monetary policy of the United States is made by the Federal Open Market Committee, which is comprised of the Board of Governors of the Federal Reserve System and the Reserve bank presidents. Twice a year the Federal Reserve Board submits a Monetary Policy Report to Congress. The most important goal of the Federal Reserve Board, in terms of its monetary policy, is to ensure that the economy grows neither too slowly or too fast. An economy that grows too quickly can lead to inflation. An economy that grows too slowly, on the other hand, can lead to a recession.**

Alan Greenspan began his fourth four-year term as Chairman of the Board of Governors of the Fed in 2000.

that banks in all 50 states must follow, and enforces those rules; the goal of the rules is to ensure that the banks are run profitably and fairly. The FDIC has its own reserves and can borrow from the U.S. Treasury.

> The Federal Deposit Insurance Corporation was founded during the Great Depression to give bank customers protection in the case of failure. A wave of bank failures brought chaos to the nation's economy during this period, and many depositors lost their money.

Federal Reserve System

See page 44

fee

A charge for professional services, such as those provided by a doctor or lawyer. A fee can also be an amount designated by a governmental body for certain kinds of filing and registration.

financing

A loan, typically secured by some kind of property as **collateral**. The loan makes possible some other purchase (for instance a car, a building, or a piece of equipment).

REAL LIFE: When you buy something, such as a car, and borrow the money to pay for it, you are said to be financing it.

fixed cost

An amount that you must pay regularly to run your business, no matter how much or how little business you do. This can include **rent**, **interest** on loans, **insurance**, and other costs. Unlike **variable costs**, fixed costs do not change as a result of a business's activity. See also **variable cost**

fixed rate

A rate of interest on a loan that will remain the same for a set period of time, no matter how interest rates change in the marketplace.

forecast

A prediction of future economic activity or performance. Forecasts may be based on many different types of reports and technical information. **Stock** market forecasters use many different reports of federal and private agencies to predict whether certain stocks will increase or decrease in value. **Sales** forecasts from particular companies are likely to be based on the company's recent sales performance combined with its assessment of future market conditions.

A man signs a document to secure a loan for a new car. The woman seated across from him helped with the financing.

foreclosure

A way that banks and other **creditors** can get all or some of their money back when a borrower does not pay as previously agreed on a **mortgage** loan. When that happens, the courts will allow a lender to assume the rights to the property and cut off the borrower's rights in and to the property.

Sometimes, payment of money owed will stop the foreclosure, even if the owner of the property is late with the payment. Sometimes it will not. After assuming **title** to the property, the lender can sell it to get its money back. If upon sale of the property, the lender cannot get all of its money back, they may impose a deficiency judgment on the property. This means that the borrower is charged with paying the difference.

fraud

Purposely taking something that belongs to someone else (typically money) by telling a lie about what will be received or delivered in an **exchange**. Fraud is a crime.

REAL LIFE: If you get a high **price** for selling a car that you know to be a modern replica by telling the buyer that it is a rare antique, you have committed fraud.

free enterprise system

See page 47

friendly takeover

Acquisition of, or **merger** with, another company, whose board of directors recommends the sale or merger. This is generally based on the fact that the board of directors believe the acquiring company is paying a fair price for the **shares** of the target company. In the case of a friendly takeover, the acquiring company will keep the managers of the target company in their present positions.

Two men shake hands as a friendly takeover between their companies is settled.

FTP (File Transfer Protocol)

This is the way that files from one computer are sent to, or retrieved from, another computer over the **Internet**. People and businesses use FTP to send files from one physical location to another. Businesses may use the system to transfer records of **sales** and purchases, customer **databases**, and so on. FTP has allowed many workers more flexibility. If an employee has a computer at home, he or she can receive and send files between the office and home.

futures

A futures **contract** is an **agreement** to buy something in the future. This kind of agreement usually applies to either a **commodity** or a **security** that will be bought for a specific price, with the **transaction** to be executed on a specific date. Once the futures agreement is made, the buyer must buy the commodity and the seller must sell it. This is different from an **option**, where the purchaser buys the right, but not the obligation, to purchase the commodity. See also **commodity**, **option**

free enterprise system

An economic system that enables individuals to make independent choices about their own **capital**, and assume both the **risks** and the rewards connected with those choices. The free enterprise system accepts an individual's right to own property; it also accepts the idea that people can own the materials necessary to create **goods** and **services** that other people may be willing to buy. Under this system, individuals or shareholders can own businesses, and the profits from those businesses are the property of the business owners. In theory, the free enterprise system allows for unrestricted buying and selling in the marketplace.

> The free enterprise system is based on certain basic principles: freedom of choice, the right of all individuals to own property, the right of owners of property to try to win profits from that property, and the right of owners of property to make their own business decisions.

One of the most important features of the free enterprise system is the property owner's right to make independent decisions about purchases, **sales**, and the manner in which businesses will be structured or run.

REAL LIFE: "Free enterprise" affects both buyers and sellers. If you want to buy a pair of blue jeans, you, as the **consumer**, are free to choose which pair has the best style, the best fit, and the best **price**, and under the free enterprise system you can make your choice from among a huge selection of jeans. A blue jean's manufacturer will be free to compete with other producers of jeans—in terms of style, size, price, and any number of other factors—to attract **customers**, secure a profit, and maintain a position in the marketplace.

G-H

goods

An inclusive term meaning all products in the marketplace. A pound of butter and a bicycle are both goods within the meaning of the term. Goods are physical, tangible products that satisfy a **consumer's** wants and needs. The term is contrasted with **services**.

A woman does her grocery shopping at the supermarket. All of the products in her basket and on the store shelves are considered goods.

guarantee

A promise that a **transaction** will be satisfying, with the understanding that the person receiving the guarantee can receive some kind of benefit or **refund** if there is a problem. There are many types of guarantees, including money-back guarantees. A financial guarantee has a slightly different application. It might mean that if you don't have the money to pay for something you agree to purchase, someone else (say, your rich uncle) would promise to pay the seller. Your wealthy uncle would then be called the guarantor.

REAL LIFE: If you sell a new kind of laundry detergent by offering a money-back guarantee, you are promising that the consumer can receive his or her money back if there's any problem with the product. You may decide to ask that the consumer meet some kind of condition to be eligible for the guarantee (for instance, returning a "proof of purchase" coupon printed on the back of the package). Guarantees can be powerful purchase incentives for consumers.

home page

The main, or first, page of a **Web site**. This is the page you land on when you type in the site's main address; it usually offers a general idea of what makes the site interesting and what else is available. Visitors can move to other pages of interest from this page. Usually, when

users click on an image, a button, or an underlined or highlighted word that explains what else can be found on the site.

In the case of a commercial site, the home page is similar to the entrance to a department store. Once you are inside, there is a directory that tells what different parts are offered. You go to the different departments to find what you want. Potential **customers** visiting a home page require quick and compelling reasons to keep reading—rather than clicking away to some other site.

HTML (HyperText Markup Language)

A relatively simple programming language used to display images to users of the **World Wide Web**. HTML is a series of commands that are retrieved and carried out by a Web browser, like Microsoft Explorer or Netscape. When you search the Web for research or to find pictures HTML translates the site's HTML code into pages of text or pictures.

> To see the HTML code in on a given Web page, just select the "View Code" option on your browser.

HTTP (HyperText Transfer Protocol)

A fast way to transfer files from the World Wide Web to your computer from the **servers** where the files reside. Think of HTTP as a cannon that shoots pages to your computer when you press "download." HTTP makes the viewing of pages on the Web possible; the characters "http://" come before Web site addresses.

human resources

The people a company pays to do work. A company's employees are essential to the company's success; so, depending on the size of the company, there is usually a director or a whole department responsible for helping to attract, hire, train, and keep the best possible staff.

The human resources department maintains hiring and firing information and oversees a range of administrative work affecting the people who work at the company. For instance, it keeps track of employee **benefits**, such as health **insurance**, sick days, vacation days, and other matters that have to do with the employees' relationship to the company. People in human resources may also have important work to do in the areas of training, **performance appraisal**, access to facilities, and maintaining a harmonious work environment. All of this work is meant to help the company make the most of its human resources.

A company's human resources department is in charge of overseeing the recruiting, hiring, and training of all new employees.

> "Commitment and passion are the only prerequisites to being an entrepreneur."
> —Kathryn Welsh

activist entrepreneur

At the age of twenty-three, Kathryn Welsh founded Bluestockings, New York City's only women's bookstore. After moving to New York in 1997, Kathryn learned that there was no women's bookstore. So, she came up with the idea of creating a bookstore, café, and community resource center, with nightly events and readings by women performers and writers. Kathryn traveled the country, visiting independent bookstores to gather advice and financial backing. On April 2, 1999, she opened Bluestockings.

Since shortly after its opening, Bluestockings has been run largely by a small paid staff and volunteers, offering their time to a wide variety of things including a reading series, a monthly art show, community outreach, and anti-racism and other workshops. As an entrepreneur who wanted to create a collectively run business, Kathryn saw firsthand the challenges of maintaining a volunteer-based staff while keeping the bookstore up and running. Nonetheless, Kathryn saw the business through three successful years, during which time the store was featured in such places as *Jane*, *The Village Voice*, *Feminist Bookstore News*, *Sojourner*, *Time Out New York*, *Bust* magazine, and *The New York Times*.

Kathryn sold Bluestockings in the winter of 2003. In the Fall of 2003, she enrolled at Harvard University to earn her MBA.

To find out more: Log on to www.bluestockings.com

POTENT QUOTES

HIGH POINTS OF RUNNING THE BUSINESS:
"Watching an idea come to life."

LOW POINTS OF RUNNING THE BUSINESS:
"The endless possibilities of a business can lead to endless exhaustion. Planning, pacing, and then pursuing is critical."

SAGE ADVICE:
"Don't let 'not knowing how' stop you! Commitment and passion are the only prerequisites to being an entrepreneur."

I

income tax

A **tax** imposed directly on the profits of companies and on the incomes of individuals. The federal government and most state governments collect these taxes. The amount that a person or business must pay is often figured out in a complicated way. Certain **expenses** (called **deductions**) can be excluded from income before the taxes are taken out. Businesses often work hard to itemize and write off everything they possibly can to reduce their taxes. Then, depending on whether a business is a **corporation** or not, the tax rate differs. In some cases a corporation's profits may be taxed, and then, when the profits are distributed to the shareholders, they are taxed a second time. In the case of smaller corporations (called **S corporations**), the profits are taxed only after they are distributed. There are advantages and disadvantages to both types of corporations, and companies usually ask the advice of **accountants** and lawyers to help them decide which type of corporation is the best for tax purposes.

A major tax issue for family-run businesses is the so-called "death tax," or inheritance tax. When a business is passed down from generation to generation, the federal government takes a large chunk of money for estate taxes. Under the administration of President George W. Bush, the inheritance tax has been repealed until 2010. It is scheduled to return in 2011.

incorporation

The process of becoming a formally recognized corporation. It is one of the duties of a state to give companies the right to operate as a corporation. The main reason companies incorporate is to protect the owners, or **shareholders**, from being personally responsible for business **debts** of the corporation (called **liabilities**). When a business is incorporated in the United States, the corporation must use the following variations in its official name: Inc. (incorporated), Corp. (corporation), LL or Ltd. (limited liability or limited). Under the law, the corporation is treated as if it is one single person.

REAL LIFE: Suppose that Joseph, Eric, and Phyllis formed a corporation in the state of Massachusetts, called JEP, Inc., and JEP, Inc. borrowed $10,000 from First National Bank of Massachusetts. After three years, JEP, Inc. can't pay the money back as promised. First National Bank of Massachusetts can sue only JEP, Inc., not Joseph, Eric, or Phyllis individually. If JEP, Inc. can't pay the bank, then First National won't be paid.

independent contractor

A self-employed person who offers **services** on a part-time or full-time basis. This work is performed under a **contract** for services, and the person who performs the job is not an employee of the person or company paying for the work. The company doesn't withhold money for **taxes** or Social Security payments for an independent contractor. It is up to the independent contractor to report his or her **earnings** in these areas to the **Internal Revenue Service** (IRS), and to handle any other administrative details related to the work.

Small business owners often turn to independent contractors for help if they need part-time or temporary help. Employees require far more legal obligations than independent contractors. However, if a small business pays an independent contractor more than $600 in a calendar year, the business is obligated to report his or her earnings to the IRS in a 1099-MISC form.

REAL LIFE: A good example of an independent contractor might be a plumber who comes to your house to fix a leaky faucet. Even though that plumber is doing work for you, he is not your employee. He works for himself and performs services (plumbing) for others. A common example of a person who does work for a company as an independent contractor might be an **accountant** who comes in once a year to go over the financial records of a company and to prepare tax returns—but who is not employed by the company.

infringement

A term used in an area of the law known as "**intellectual property**." Intellectual property includes **patents**, **trademarks**, **service marks**, and **copyrights**. These are rights given to people who register them and claim an exclusive right in them. If you own any of these types of

A plumber repairs a problem. He is an independent contractor that works for himself.

intellectual property rights, and someone else tries to use them, the person using what you own is said to infringe on your rights. See also **intellectual property**

REAL LIFE: If Brogan opens a business making soft drinks and gives her drinks the name "Coca Cola," she might get a lot of business right away because of name recognition, but she would be infringing on the Coca Cola company's trademark. If Erin writes a great song, but without permission has taken the words directly from a CD by singer Avril Lavigne, she is infringing on Lavigne's copyright.

insurance

The act of insuring things, people, or business against some kind of harm or **loss**. Insurance is a binding **contract** that requires an insurance company to provide compensation for a specified damage, **loss**, or injury suffered, in return for a premium (a sum of money) paid to that company.

There are many types of insurance. The purpose of insurance is to protect someone against some kind of loss. Life insurance, for instance, protects against loss of life. Of course, this doesn't mean insurance can keep you from dying; it means that the insurance company will pay your **beneficiary** (usually a surviving husband or wife, and/or children) some amount of money to help

> The success of any business is dependent on hard work and ingenuity. However, no matter how dedicated you are, one disaster can wipe out everything. The key to making sure that the time and money you've invested doesn't vanish if disaster strikes is to protect it with the proper insurance.

financially make up for your death. Property and casualty insurance protects against loss of property. For example, if a company's **manufacturing** plant burns down, the company that purchased the right insurance policy can be reimbursed (that is, can collect money) for the loss by the insurance company. The insurance company makes money to cover these payments—and makes a profit—by collecting premiums (payments from policyholders) and investing them. Insurance is also referred to as indemnity or coverage. See also **liability insurance**

Homeowner's insurance protects against damage to property, such as in the case of a fire. Life insurance provides protection for family members in case of death. All car owners are required to carry car insurance by law, in the event of a traffic accident.

insurance

See page 53

intellectual property

Trade secrets, recipes and top-secret formulas, and manuscripts all fall under the intellectual property category. Intellectual property includes whatever thoughts separate a company from its competitors. These thoughts that make a company unique are essentially interpreted as assets. Scripts, screenplays, and other written material should be copyrighted, and name **brands** and slogans should be trademarked in order to be protected. See also **copyright**, **service mark**, and **trademark**

> In some industries intellectual property makes up as much as 90 percent of a company's assets. The entertainment and software industries are both prime examples of this type of field. It is crucial if you work in either field to do whatever you can to protect all intellectual property, because if someone tries to steal an idea, there is no legal recourse but to prove that you have taken steps to protect your idea.

A woman works on a top-secret formula (intellectual property) in a pharmaceutical lab.

insolvent

Incapable of meeting financial commitments. When a company does not have enough money (or valuable **assets** that can be turned into **cash** to pay its bills), the company is said to be insolvent. On the other hand, if a company has a lot of heavy machinery, **real estate**, or other assets that are not easily sold but are valued at more than the amount of its **debts**, that firm is not insolvent; it is simply not liquid. (A liquid asset is one that can be sold easily and quickly, like **stocks** and **bonds**.)

interest

1. The **price** you pay for using someone else's money. When you borrow money, the individual or bank that lends the money typically expects to make something extra back for lending you the money. (This is why people go into the business of lending money in the first place!) Interest is usually charged at a certain **rate** or percentage of the loan for a certain period of time.

2. A portion of control in property or a business. Someone who has an interest in a company has part ownership, or a **share**, of the property or business.

interest rate

The amount or percentage of money that a borrower pays, over and above what he or she borrows, for the privilege of using the money. If you borrow $10 from Jim, and he charges 10 percent **interest** per month, you will have to pay Jim $11 if you pay back the loan next month. ($10 plus 10 percent of $10, or $1=$11.) Jim gets back his $10 and makes a profit of 10 percent, or $1.

Internal Revenue Service
(IRS)

An agency of the federal government; a division of the Department of the Treasury. The IRS's main purpose is the collection of federal **income taxes** from individuals and companies. Another job of the IRS is to conduct tax **audits**—that is, check individual tax returns to make sure that people and organizations have paid the proper amount. Avoiding audits (and the possibility of penalties or prosecution for the underpayment of taxes) is a significant incentive for people and organizations to avoid breaking tax laws.

Internet

Often referred to as the Information Superhighway; the system by which millions of individual computers around the globe can communicate with one another. The Internet offers vast amounts of information, through the **World Wide Web**, that any computer user can access through browsers on their own computers. The World Wide Web is a network of users who can exchange information, **e-mail**, and files with one another through visually oriented pages (**Web sites**). The Internet has changed the way we do business. Business meetings and overnight deliveries are diminished thanks to e-mail. Through the Internet, businesses of any size can market themselves by creating their own Web site. See also **FTP**, **HTML**, and **HTTP**

inventory

An amount of **goods**, usually of what a company sells, that is kept on hand to fill orders. The more of a product a company keeps on hand, the larger the inventory. There are advantages and disadvantages to having a large inventory. The advantages include having enough on hand to meet fast **delivery** requirements for your **customers**. The disadvantages include having money tied up in goods that might or might not sell, and having to allocate space that could be used for other purposes. In other words, high inventory is convenient, but that convenience comes at a cost, one of which is your company's ability to buy new products. If the **price** of your inventory goes down because the **demand** drops, or if your competitor comes out with a more competitive offering, then you may find yourself at a disadvantage.

Hundreds of watches are kept on hand as inventory in a watch store.

investment

An opportunity for people or companies to make money by supplying their own money. An investment might be a new company a friend or relative starts; it may be the purchase of **securities**; it might involve buying a business property. In any investment, the money is always handed over in the expectation that the **investor** will get more back than he or she put in. (This does not, of course, always happen—investing is an inherently risky activity.)

REAL LIFE: If your brother-in-law asks you for $5,000 to start a new company, and promises you 50 percent of the profits in return, the request for $5,000 represents an investment opportunity for you. If you decide to give your brother-in-law the money, you would have made an investment—and assumed the risk that the business would not succeed.

> "Never invest your money in anything that eats or needs repairing."
>
> — Billy Rose, composer

investor

A person or company who places money in another enterprise, or **security**, in order to make more money. Investors operate in virtually all industries, and are motivated by a wide variety of different philosophies. Investors do not typically participate in the daily operation of a business, but instead play a passive role.

invoice

A bill for **goods** or **services**. An invoice generally includes a date, the type of goods or services purchased, the amount per unit or element, and a total amount. An invoice often provides the day the bill has to be paid, and describes any **discount** for early payment.

> It's always a good idea to follow up with a phone call to confirm that your invoice was received. You might want to wait a couple of weeks before you make the call, but it's certainly not worth waiting a month or two, only to find out that your invoice was never received.

Due to the risky nature of some investments, it's wise to monitor them closely. The woman above checks her investments over the phone.

jobber

A "middleman," typically someone who buys from **wholesalers** and sells to **retailers**. Whereas large retailers can often buy **merchandise** directly from wholesalers, many wholesalers will not sell small amounts to small retailers. A jobber is able to buy large quantities at a lower **price** and then sell them in smaller portions to smaller retailers at a higher price. The jobber fulfills a need in the **market** and takes a smaller percentage than a wholesaler might. The large **volume** of smaller retailers who may buy his **goods** usually makes up for the smaller margin.

joint venture

When two or more businesses join together on a project. Although joint ventures are common in business, they do not necessarily translate into a legal bond between the two businesses. Joint ventures generally fall into three different categories—a **partnership** joint venture, a contractual joint venture, and an **investment** joint venture. It's important for businesses to be specific with each other about which type of joint venture they are forming.

A partnership joint venture describes a situation in which two companies each contribute essential assets to the venture. For example, if one company contributes the production know-how necessary for the partnership, the second company would perhaps offer the marketing knowledge and experience. On the other hand, a contractual joint venture is when two companies make an **agreement** to work solely with one another, but are not in business to together. For example, a small gourmet grocery store decides to buy its organic eggs from only one farmer, or **supplier**. An investment joint venture happens when two companies join together to create a third separate company. The third company is a separate legal entity that was formed perhaps by using money from one company and an equal value's worth of property or facilities from another company for equal ownership by the two companies. See also **partnership**

junk bond

A bond with a low **credit** rating and a high **yield** is a junk bond. Junk bonds offer investors a higher risk than bonds of financially sound companies. Junk bonds are often used in corporate **takeovers** and **leveraged buyouts**. Two agencies, Standard & Poors and Moody's Investor Services, provide the rating systems for companies' credit.

law of supply and demand

Economic proposition that holds that, in a free market, the relationship between the amount of goods available and the number of **customers** for those goods will determine both the price and the quantity produced. A change in either will lead to changes in price and/or the amount produced.

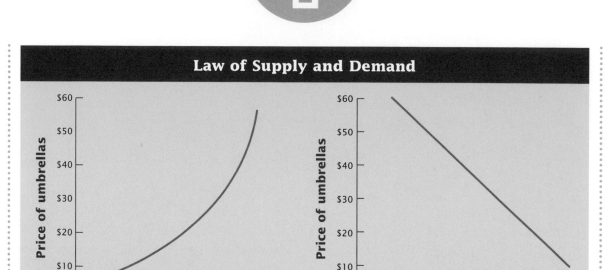

Law of Supply and Demand

Left graph: Price of umbrellas ($10–$60) vs. Quantity of umbrellas produced (supply) (0–30)

Right graph: Price of umbrellas ($10–$60) vs. Quantity of umbrellas sold (demand) (0–30)

REAL LIFE: Suppose that Walter makes umbrellas. Suppose that this month, umbrella sales drop dramatically for Walter and all of his competitors. Walter, and the other manufacturers, will be under pressure to lower the **price** of umbrellas to attract new **customers**. Therefore, they will be likely to reduce their production of umbrellas, as well. Six months later, if there were to be a sudden surge in **demand** for umbrellas, and if there were umbrella shortages at virtually all retailers, the price might well go up (because **consumers** would be willing to pay more), and Walter and his competitors might choose to increase the production of umbrellas.

lease

A way of acquiring or using something without purchasing it. Typically, businesses lease facilities or equipment; in the case of equipment, the term of the lease is often tied to the life expectancy of the item being leased. Some equipment and automobile leases give the person or organization doing the leasing (known as the lessee) the option of buying the equip-

ment at a greatly reduced rate at the end of the lease. There are certain **tax** advantages to leasing cars and equipment rather than purchasing them outright; another possible advantage over purchase is that the payments may be somewhat lower.

There are two different types of commercial leases for retail or office spaces—a gross lease and a **net** lease. A gross lease includes **taxes**, **utilities**, and the cost of **insurance** in the **rent**. A net lease is one in which the landlord pays for these costs separately.

leveraged buyout (LBO)

A way to take a public **corporation** private by **financing** through the use of **debt** funds: short-term bank loans and **bonds**. Because of the large amount of debt in comparison to **equity** in the new corporation, the bonds typically have a low rating, or are **junk bonds**. **Investors** can participate in a leveraged buyout through either buying the debt (i.e., buying the bonds or bank loan) or the purchase of equity through an LBO fund that specializes in such **investments**.

liabilities

1. In business, generally, **debts**. Most businesses carry a certain amount of loans and debts. Liabilities must be included in the company's **balance sheet**.
2. Individual responsibility or accountability taken for one's own actions, behavior, or property.

liability insurance

A kind of **insurance** that protects a person or business against an injury to another person (or his or her property) while on the insured's property. Liability insurance can also insure against claims of injury or harm related to a certain product manufactured by the company. This kind of insurance is called product liability insurance.

Sometimes a person who claims injury or harm and the insurance company argue over whether the person making the claim was careful enough, used a product properly, or really sustained significant injury or harm to warrant compensation. When this happens, the manufacturer may get sued, but in most cases the insurance company provides attorneys to defend the claim, and then pays what the court decides is a fair amount to the person filing the suit (if the court decides in favor of the person making the claim).

REAL LIFE: If you fall on my property and get hurt, my liability insurance is supposed to pay for a valid claim you make against me. If you use a water heater that my company makes, and you get seriously burned, even after you followed all the directions for the heater's use and heeded all the warnings I placed on the machine, then my liability insurance should pay for the injury you suffered.

license

1. A formal certification that allows a person or business to engage in a particular activity. Various types of businesses are regulated by the state and require licenses for people who want to operate in those businesses: doctors, lawyers, beauticians, and physical therapists, for example. Companies that want to engage in certain types of businesses—such as producing or selling liquor, or operating waste-processing facilities—are regulated in a similar way. The states have an interest in protecting citizens from people or businesses lacking the training, experience, or resources needed to operate in these areas, so they require proof that those who wish to work in such businesses or professions are competent.
2. The right to use a certain **asset** of a company (typically **intellectual property**) for an agreed upon **price** and period of time.

limited liability company (LLC)

A legal entity that is not taxable itself and distributes the profits to its owners, but limits possible **loss** to what has already been invested. A limited liability company creates a protected alternative to forming a **corporation** for small business owners. Similar to a corporation, an LLC limits the personal liability for small business owners' debts, but LLCs require far less paperwork and expenses than a corporation. An LLC provides its owner protection from being sued for personal assets—only the assets contributed to the LLC are at risk. Limited liability companies are simple and inexpensive to run in most states. When and if the time comes to turn an LLC into a corporation, the procedure is fairly easy.

liquidity

1. The ability to change assets into **cash** easily and quickly. A person's or business's liquidity

refers to the ability to raise cash in a hurry from existing resources.

2. A **market** is called "liquid" when it is at a high level of trading activity, allowing buying and selling with little price disturbance. This market is also characterized by the ability to buy and sell easily.

loan agreement

A document signed by lending and borrowing parties showing that a loan exists, and specifying the terms of the loan: the amount, the time period, the **interest rate**, and the kind of loan. A loan **agreement** spells out what happens if the borrower fails to pay, and state laws that govern any litigation that may ultimately be brought. Businesses typically hire lawyers to review the language of loan agreements closely.

Bank officers and clients review and sign papers for a loan agreement.

loss

The situation you face when **expenses** are more than your income. It is the opposite of a profit, where your income exceeds your expenses. A loss also occurs when you buy something (say, **stock** or **inventory**) for a certain **price** and the price later goes down. This kind of loss doesn't become a formal loss until you have to sell at the lower price. If the value has gone down, but you are not forced to sell it, the loss is called a **paper loss**.

A shoe sale attracts a potential customer. The store lures consumers with sale prices in hopes they'll buy additional full-priced products.

loss leader

A **marketing** idea designed to increase overall sales by prominently offering a single product or **service** at a **loss** (or a substantial **discount**). This strategy has been strongly connected with the **retail** industry, but it has been applied to many other areas of business as well. The idea is to build **consumer** confidence and entice **customers** who are interested in the loss leader (or discounted product) to purchase additional products or services. Loss leaders are generally heavily advertised; their basic goal in a retail setting is to increase foot traffic within the store.

mailing list

A specifically predetermined list, usually used in **direct mail** selling, featuring people that the mailer believes would be likely to be interested in purchasing the products or **services** advertised. These lists are generally aimed at narrowly defined groups. Businesses often sell their mailing lists to other businesses. A return of 1 to 2 percent is considered a success in many direct mail campaigns.

Mailing lists that consist of people who have recently purchased products or services similar to yours may deliver better purchase totals than other lists.

management

1. People who run a company or organization on a day-to-day basis, and who also determine long-range policies for the organization.

A company's management team

marketing

The processes and strategies that bring companies together with the **customers** they hope to reach. In daily use, the word "marketing" is often distinguished from "**sales**" because marketing executives often have important decisions to make about identifying, **positioning**, and promoting products that salespeople do not face. As a practical matter, though, "marketing" describes a huge portion of what a company must do to stay in business (namely, turn a profit by selling products and **services** to customers), and a certain amount of

Madame C. J. Walker
(1867–1919)

overlap between the two ideas is inevitable. One of the best formal definitions of marketing comes from the American Marketing Association: "The process of planning and executing the conception, pricing, **promotion** and distribution of ideas, **goods**, and **services** to create **exchanges** that satisfy individual and organizational objectives." In other words, marketing is figuring out what you have to do to get people to buy from you or work with you—and then doing that. There are many ways to market a company's goods or services, including face-to-face selling, telesales, broadcast **advertising**, **public relations**, and **Internet** campaigns, among many other possibilities. Other important marketing issues that precede the selling process include the development of a certain product or service, its pricing, its packaging, and the choice of **distribution channels**. (Will the product or service be sold through **retail** stores? Via mail order? In specialty stores? At industry **trade shows**? Through small gatherings in individual homes, hosted by a local distributor?)

> Madame C. J. Walker was an important pioneer in American marketing. Born Sarah Breedlove, Walker marketed her line of hair-care products by means of an innovative army of uniformed salespeople, known as "Walker Agents." These agents made their way from home to home in black neighborhoods, followed Walker's detailed selling system, and bought products from her company. Walker, an African-American, was among the first women to become a millionaire as an entrepreneur. At one point, she directly employed three thousand people and provided incomes for an estimated twenty thousand Walker Agents.

The term generally includes the chief executive officer, the financial officers, the board of directors, the organization's department managers, and so on. As a group, people within management are sometimes referred to as executives, and may be distinguished from other employees (labor).

2. The act or task of running a company or setting its course.

manufacturing

The process of making things for sale. The word is usually used to refer to items that are produced in large quantities and that are similar or identical.

margin

Usually, the difference between a company's **net** sales and the cost of the **merchandise** it has sold. (The term is also used in investing to describe a method of purchasing **stock**.)

market

1. An organized gathering of traders.

2. The group of potential **customers** for a given product or **service**. Historically, the market, or marketplace, was a physical, public place where people came together and bought and sold their wares. In today's terms, the market is any area of the economy where **goods** and services are traded, and the trading may well take place between people who are hundreds or thousands of miles apart. In the **securities** market, **stocks** and **bonds** are traded. There are specialized markets for food, home furnishings, clothing, housing, automobiles, and virtually any other product or service you can possibly think of. When people speak in the abstract of

A market can be a financial trading place, such as the New York Stock Exchange, a mall where several stores or "markets" are found, or a more traditional type of market like the farmers market shown above.

"the market," the odds are good that they're talking about the stock market as a whole.

market forecast

A projection of the size, preferences, and trends within a target **market**. Entrepreneurs develop market **forecasts** to get an idea of how many **customers** there are in a given target market for a product or **service**, and how likely those customers are to buy. Other projections about markets try to tell entrepreneurs why particular customers make the purchase decisions they do, and how various customer groups break down.

market share

The percentage of **sales** in a particular industry or market that a company or product enjoys.

REAL LIFE: If you wanted to determine the domestic market share for the competing soft-drink products Diet Fizz and Diet Bubbly, you might first look at the market for all diet drinks by asking, "How much diet soda did Americans drink last year?" Suppose you learn from an **Internet** search that the answer was 40 million cases—and that Diet Fizz accounted for 10 million of those cases, more than anyone else. Diet Bubbly, you learn, sold 8 million cases, and was in second place. Diet Fizz would be the market-share leader in that segment of the soft-drink market, with 25 percent of the diet-soda sales nationwide. Diet Fizz would be the runner-up with 20 percent of the diet-soda sales.

market targeting

Choosing a part of a market to try to sell to. When an entrepreneur or company evaluates different segments of the market, and then chooses one or more of the market segments to compete in, that process is known as market targeting. When marketing to **consumers**, companies typically target groups defined by

factors like age, gender, income, or educational level (**demographics**). Once a market segment has been targeted, the company must select a marketing tool that reaches and can deliver responses from the group targeted. See also **marketing mix**

market value

1. The best **price** a seller can get for a product or service that may be sold in the future. If an item has not been appraised prior to sale, its fair market value is the amount a willing buyer will pay and a willing seller will sell it for. The market value of a **stock** or **bond** is the current price at which it is trading.

2. The given value **investors** believe a company is worth. This value is calculated by multiplying the number of outstanding **shares** by the current market price of the company's shares.

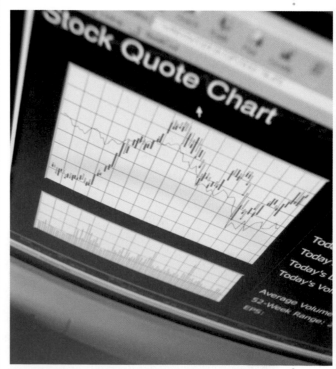

Stockholders often check the current price at which their stock is trading to find out what the market value is. This helps investors determine when to sell or buy.

marketing

See page 62

A **salesperson uses** fabric samples as marketing materials to attract a potential customer.

marketing materials

Materials that are provided to help sell products or **services**. They are typically used by salespeople, but may be meant to work independently to attract **customer** inquiries or secure orders, as in the case of "Take One" brochures set up in display stands in public areas. These days, a company's **Web site** is usually considered an important element of its marketing material mix.

marketing mix

An organization's total offer to prospective customers. The marketing mix encompasses all four of the essential elements of a **marketing** effort: product, **price**, placement/distribution, and **promotion**.

marketing research

An attempt to determine the size and direction of the **market** for a given product or service—and, often, whether a market exists in the first place. Marketing research is typically conducted by gathering information about the size and structure of the potential market, and by conducting tests that help to determine whether or not the product will be successful. This kind of research may be employed well before the product is developed, and it often continues until it reaches **consumers**.

> One man considered to be an early innovator in the field of marketing research was Cecil "Bud" Phillips, a Texas advertising executive who helped bring attention to the field in the 1950s, and who stayed active in marketing research for the next four decades. His motto was, "Find out what people want…and make it for them." Phillips provided expert analysis of consumer markets for companies such as Borden—predicting, for instance, that demand for ice cream from shoppers would support a campaign to install freezers in grocery stores. He was right. Before Phillips came along, big companies "played hunches" about the markets they were trying to reach, and often regretted having done so. After Phillips, a more scientific approach—involving ongoing polls of statistically representative groups of people within target markets—was the order of the day.

mentor

A trusted guide and overseer, typically one working with a younger and less experienced person. The name comes from the Greek liter-

Automaker Henry Ford's mentor was the famed inventor Thomas Alva Edison.

ary figure Mentor, whom Homer described in the *Odyssey* as the "wise and trusted counselor." Odysseus asked Mentor to watch over his home while he was away. In the story, the goddess Athena took on Mentor's likeness when she protected and taught Telemachus, Odysseus's son. Today, the term refers to a seasoned, experienced person who helps to guide the progress and development of another. Mentors are common in business settings, and most successful entrepreneurs develop important relationships with senior advisors. Effective mentoring might include showing someone how to talk to potential **customers**, how to keep good business records, how to keep costs down, how to deal with customer complaints, and any of a thousand other topics.

merchandise

1. **Goods** and **commodities** sold to the public; also, **inventory**.

2. To sell goods and merchandise in a specific way. The term "merchandising" may refer to the way goods are creatively displayed or advertised to prospective **consumers**, or to the ordering and pricing strategies used to increase **sales**. **Retail** businesses are utterly dependent on the success of their merchandising abilities. Merchandise must be both displayed beautifully and be easily accessible to the customer.

merchant account

A special bank account maintained by a merchant in order to receive **credit** card payments. The account is often linked by telephone or an **online service** to verify the accounts of customers with a central office. Establishing a merchant account is an essential step in setting up a retail or online business, since consumers in both of these channels often purchase goods using a credit card.

merchant bank

A British term that in the United States is more commonly referred to as an **investment** bank. A merchant bank specializes not in lending out its own funds, but in providing various financial **services**, such as advising companies on new **stock** and accepting **liability** for these newly issued stocks. Merchant, or investment, banks also offer advice on **acquisitions**, **mergers**, foreign exchange, **portfolio** management, etc.

merger

The process by which the businesses of two similar-sized companies are combined. There are a number of different ways for this to take place. Usually, a merger is a **tax**-free transaction.

mission statement

A written explanation of your company's purpose. A mission statement lays the groundwork for how you run your company. It can take the form of a simple sentence or a paragraph.

A **borrower reviews** the mortgage he has secured to help finance a new home.

> "To experience the emotion of competition, winning and crushing the competitors."
>
> —mission statement by Nike

monopoly

See page 69

mortgage

An arrangement that is secured by **collateral** and gives a lender an **interest** in something, typically **real estate**, owned by a person or company that owes the lender money. The borrower makes a predetermined series of payments. If the borrower fails to repay, the lender can appeal to a court to order the sale of the property in order to raise money to repay the loan. This process is known as **foreclosure**. Mortgages, with varying **interest rates**, generally run between 10 and 30 years, during which time the loan is to be paid off.

REAL LIFE: Assume that Jim owns a large piece of construction equipment, and he wants to obtain **financing** to expand his construction business. Jim might choose to arrange a mortgage, which would mean giving a local bank a document placing a lien—or restriction—on the equipment as **security** for the repayment of the **debt**. This would mean that the construction equipment could not be sold until the lien was paid off. It would also mean that if Jim failed to make payments as promised, the bank could arrange to have the property sold to satisfy the lien. When the debt is paid, the lien is removed. When such a mortgage is placed on a piece of machinery or a car or truck, it is called a chattel mortgage.

multi-level marketing (MLM)

A means of selling **merchandise** that depends on both winning **customers** and attracting new distributors for the product or **service** in question. Primarily, it is used for **consumer** products sold from customers' homes by independent sellers, or distributors. Multi-level marketing is business in which a person receives profit not only from their own **sales**, but from the sales made by people they have signed up, and the people those people have signed up, etc.

Each such seller is encouraged to develop new sellers and to manage the new sellers' sales as well as their own. In this way, distributors can make **commissions** on the sales of those they have recruited, as well as on their own sales. Since they get commissions on their customer's sales, it is in their best interest to keep recruiting more and more salespeople. Although there are some reputable companies built on the principle of multi-level marketing, the system has attracted a good deal of criticism. Some of this criticism has to do with exaggerated and unrealistic claims about the possibility of newcomers to the system making very large sums of money within a multi-level-marketing network, which is in fact quite unlikely.

multinational

Extending across the borders of one or more countries. When a company has a business presence in more than one country, it is said to be a multinational company.

REAL LIFE: If Inez owns a company that sells and **markets** in the United States, but owns

This pie graph depicts a multinational company's profits from continents around the world.

manufacturing plants in several countries in Asia and Europe, she would be said to be the operator of a multinational company.

mutual fund

An **investment** fund managed by a professional team that contains **stocks** or **bonds** of many different companies. **Investors** can put a small amount of money into such funds, allowing them to diversify without investing a large amount of money. There are many different kinds of funds: stock funds, bond funds, **futures** funds, and global funds, to name a few. The kind of fund an investor might buy is determined by his/her investment goals. Some funds, for example, are meant to generate income on a regular basis, while other mutual funds seek to protect an investor's money. Still others seek to invest in companies that are growing at a rapid pace. Funds often impose a sales charge on investors when they buy or sell **shares**. Many funds these days, however, impose no sales charge. Mutual funds are investment companies that became regulated by the Investment Company Act of 1940.

monopoly

A situation where a business has no meaningful **competition** for its product or **service**. Businesses with monopolies are in a position to charge almost any **price** they wish; the potentially harmful effects of such business operations led to the passage of two important pieces of legislation designed to limit anti-competitive business in the United States. The Sherman Antitrust Act (passed in 1890) prohibits the restraint of interstate or foreign trade; the Clayton Antitrust Act (passed in 1914) regulates practices that may undercut competition in the marketplace, including **mergers** and **acquisitions**, price discrimination, **contracts** that promote exclusive dealing, and overlapping leadership between companies.

Famed businessman and monopolist J. P. Morgan stands holding the American flag.

"Monopoly-busting," under the authority of the 1890 and 1914 antitrust acts, has had an up-and-down history in the United Sates. President Theodore Roosevelt used the Sherman Antitrust Act to challenge the economic empires of J. P. Morgan and John D. Rockefeller; Rockefeller's Standard Oil Company was divided into 30 different companies. The antitrust laws helped keep big companies from becoming "too big" (however that was defined at any given time) through mergers and acquisitions. After the 1982 breakup of AT&T's telephone monopoly, however, antitrust suits became somewhat less common. The high-profile antitrust case against **software** giant Microsoft that originated in the late 1990s at first went against the company, but Microsoft eventually reached a settlement with the Justice Department and nine states.

NASDAQ

A national **market** administered by the National Association of Securities Dealers (NASDAQ). The NASDAQ specializes in trading the stocks of newer companies and technology stocks. In order to list on the NASDAQ, a stock must comply with the rules of the **exchange** and meet certain criteria set out by the exchange.

negotiation

The process of making mutually beneficial business decisions through bargaining. Sometimes negotiations center on pricing, but other important concerns may include payment terms, **service** plans, **delivery** dates, confidentiality, or any of a number of different issues. If the parties are successful in their negotiations, they usually draw up a **contract** that spells out all the terms that they have agreed upon. A successful negotiation session usually involves each party giving up something to get something else in return.

> **Developing a successful negotiating strategy usually begins with your identifying two important things: the minimum acceptable offer (the point at which you are willing to walk away from negotiations) and the current market value of the products or services under discussion.**

net

The amount of money left after **deductions** are made from a total, or gross, amount. (These deductions from gross income totals may be for any number of things, including **discounts**, costs of **sales**, **overhead**, **taxes**, and so on.)

networking

1. Making social and business contacts with others in your industry, or other industries, partic-

A woman networks via telephone.

ularly with people who can help you. (Networking is simply "connecting to and talking to people over time" by a different name.) By developing business contacts and forming new business relationships, you can increase your knowledge, expand your business base, or better serve the community.

2. Hooking up two or more computers or other pieces of equipment so they can work together.

net worth

The amount of the value of everything you own, after all the **liabilities** (the **debts** you owe) are subtracted.

REAL LIFE: If you have a house worth $175,000, other property worth $25,000, **investments** worth $140,000, and total debts (including your home **mortgage**) of $100,000, your net worth would be $240,000.

New York Stock Exchange (NYSE)

The oldest and largest of the U.S. stock exchanges. It has been in existence since 1792 and is also known as the Big Board or simply "The Exchange." The NYSE is located at 11 Wall Street in New York City. **Common** and **preferred stocks**, **bonds**, and **options** are all traded on the floor of the NYSE. The exchange has strict requirement for **securities** to be listed on it. More than 2,000 common and preferred stocks are traded on the New York Stock Exchange.

newsgroup

A computer-accessed forum where a specialized topic is discussed by means of public messages. When a message is posted, it can be responded to by anyone who is a member of the newsgroup. Many newsgroups are found on Usenet, a global system for posting many different types of forums on various topics.

The New York Stock Exchange

On May 17, 1792, twenty four traders inaugurated the first session of what would eventually be known as the New York Stock Exchange. If you were to go to 68 Wall Street in Manhattan, you'd be standing near where they stood. The Exchange has operated continuously since then with only a few interruptions. It shut down briefly in 1873 because of economic turmoil; for half of 1914 during World War I; for a week and a half in 1933 as part of the "bank holiday" meant to ease Depression-era financial jitters; and for four days in September 2001, following terrorist attacks on the United States.

These antique glass bottles are a niche because they attract only a select group of buyers.

newsletter

A document, usually circulated among members of an interested group, within a company, or within an industry, that tells the news of the particular group for which it is written. In a **corporation**, newsletters often feature information about employees, recent work initiatives, and topics of interest to those who work for the company. Within an industry newsletter, the topics tend to be of greater interest to **management** than to employees, since these newsletters typically focus on business trends within the industry.

niche

A small segment of a **market** targeted for an exclusive type of product or **service**. See also **niche marketing**

niche marketing

Efforts to win **customers** within a fairly narrow portion of a larger group of potential buyers. Niche marketing sometimes focuses on segments of markets that feature high profitability and/or minimal **competition**.

REAL LIFE: If Joan develops a line of clothes made without leather or any other animal products, and markets her products successfully to people who are concerned about animal cruelty, Joan has built a position in a niche market within the larger market of clothes buyers.

not-for-profit organization

An incorporated organization that is typically created for educational or charitable purposes, and from which no shareholders or trustees gain financially.

note

A written promise to pay a **debt**. The note could be in the form of a document that states the amount of the debt, the date the loan was made, and the promise by the debtor to pay by a certain date.

REAL LIFE: If Joseph loans Helen money and writes down how much he loans her, when he makes the loan, when the loan is due, and outlines Helen's promise to pay by that date, and Helen then signs that document, Helen has made a note to Joseph.

notice

An official statement of legal action or intent to take a legal action. If a tenant has not paid **rent**, he or she may receive a notice of eviction.

> "I pretty much make it clear to all of my customers that I am 13. I think they know by the way I talk on the phone."
>
> —Eitan Feinberg

computer whiz

At age four, Eitan Feinberg worked on his first computer. At age eleven, he launched his own company, CyproX, from his Mercer Island, Washington, home. The company builds highly customized computers and does Web design for its customers. CyproX builds its own computers by purchasing the parts individually and assembling PCs based on consumer preference. As of this writing, Eitan is all of 13 years old—and his company is grossing in the high five figures annually! Eitan keeps the company going by typically putting in 40 hours a week. Somehow he's learned how to get his homework done at school, so he can leave time for his customers.

In order to remain in competition with the likes of the computer giants Dell, Gateway, and IBM, Eitan specializes in building machines exactly the way his customers want, and he keeps his prices quite low. He also adds extras that the big companies don't, such as a do-it-yourself option. This allows his clients to literally watch as Feinberg creates their custom computer. So far the giants like Dell, IBM, and Gateway haven't been able to match this unique special service.

To find out more: Log on to www.cyprox.com

POTENT QUOTES

HIGH POINTS OF RUNNING THE BUSINESS:

"I got a lot of help from my father early on with tax forms and other accounting and legal details."

LOW POINTS OF RUNNING THE BUSINESS:

"A lot of people have tried to take advantage of me because I'm 13; just recently I found out about someone who was trying to rip me off."

SAGE ADVICE:

"First, make sure you can handle people; they're harder to read than any computer code. Second... support your product or service.... People have good ideas, but have no way to support what they sell."

online

A situation where one computer is connected to another computer. As a practical matter, people now use the word "online" to mean the same as "connected to the **Internet**."

online newsletter

A **newsletter** transmitted via **e-mail** or some other means of electronic transmission, rather than on paper.

online service

A **service** that provides access to the Internet, **e-mail**, news, electronic forums, and a variety of others. Online services differ from Internet service providers (ISPs) because ISPs generally provide only connection to the Internet and a few basic services (such as e-mail). You might say that an online service is a place to visit and to find places of interest, whereas an ISP provides a way to go to other places. America Online is an example of an online service.

operating costs

The costs generally associated with running a business. These costs, also known as operating expenses, might include the cost of electricity and other utilities, costs of labor, and costs of the **goods** necessary in **manufacturing**.

Operating costs can also include **debt**, **rent**, **advertising**, and so on. **Overhead** is included in operating costs.

option

1. An extra that one might add, for a **price**, when purchasing a product, such as a car. (A sunroof might be an option in a car purchase.) 2. A right, but not the obligation, a purchaser pays for to buy or sell an **asset** at a set price at a later date. If that purchaser changes his/her mind, he/she doesn't have to go through with the purchase, but does have to pay for the seller reserving the right to him/her. Investors, not companies, issue **options**. Investors who purchase call options bet that **stock** will be worth more than the price set by the option, plus the price they paid for the option itself.

REAL LIFE: Suppose Emma wants to buy a building for her retail business. She knows the location is perfect. The seller is asking a high price—more than she can pay at this time. Emma is expecting a big sale at a big profit, and is also negotiating with banks for better **financing** terms. She is willing to pay the seller a sum of $10,000 for an exclusive right, or option, to buy the property within one year. If all the things she's waiting for work out, then she will exercise her option and pay the seller his price. If not, she has lost her $10,000, but she hasn't obligated herself to purchase a building that she can't afford after all.

An outsourced computer programmer works on developing a new software for a company.

outsourcing

Paying another person or business to take responsibility for one of the processes of your business (such as handling incoming calls from new **customers**, or developing a new kind of **software**, or producing parts your company assembles into finished products). Outsourcing can simplify a company's operations or result in cost savings, or both. It can also, on occasion, lead to internal communications or work-flow problems. Kinds of **services** commonly outsourced are payroll, **taxes**, and **advertising**.

> Outsourcing is relied on so heavily in the business world that there is an organization, called the Outsourcing Institute, dedicated solely to bringing people and businesses together.

overhead

Costs that must be paid to keep a business running. These costs are not directly related to things like buying the supplies to make a product, but are the day-to-day expenses, such as the cost of labor, **rent**, utilities, **insurance**, **marketing**, and workers' **benefits**. In setting **prices**, business decision makers usually try to distribute these costs within each sale, so that prices account for overhead and still leave room for a healthy profit.

A few ways businesses diminish overhead costs are to share office space, or by hiring temporary workers. Other simple but important ways to cut down on overhead are always to go with the most economical option, for example, use toll-free numbers when possible and use the cheapest overnight delivery service and online service.

paper loss

Loss that has happened but has not yet been realized through a transaction, such as a **stock** that has fallen in value but is still being held. Also known as an unrealized loss. See also **paper profit**

paper profit

Profit that has been made but not yet realized through a transaction, such as a stock that has risen in value but is still being held. Also known as unrealized gain or unrealized profit. See also **paper loss**

partnership

See page 78

patent

An exclusive right, granted by a government, to the inventor of a product or process to keep others from profiting from the invention. The purpose of U.S. patent law is to encourage and reward innovation that benefits others. Patents can be applied to processes, machines, pharmaceutical products, and other manufactured products of exclusive, new design. The inventor who receives a patent is assured that his product cannot legally be copied, made or sold by others without permission for the life of the patent. U.S. patents last for seventeen years from the date the patent is granted, or twenty years from when it is first filed. After the patent has expired, the invention becomes **public**

domain, which means that anyone can make, use, or sell the invention.

Patents are typically filed in one country only, so a patent granted by the United States will not protect an invention in another country. **Inventors** can, however, apply for a global patent offered under the Patent Cooperation Treaty of 1978, overseen by the World Intellectual Property Organization (WIPO). The WIPO is based in Geneva, Switzerland. See also **copyright**, **intellectual property**, **service mark**, **trademark**

payables

Money owed by a company for goods and service. See also **receivables**

pay-per-click

A method of **advertising** on the **World Wide Web**. When a **Web site** has banner or button ads, these often advertise products and **services** that are not directly connected to the host Web site. Sometimes the cost for placing these kinds of ads is a regular monthly **fee**, like **rent**. There is, however, another way to pay. In a pay-per-click **agreement**, when visitors to the site click on a button or banner, the

company that owns that advertisement pays the hosting page a certain amount. The number of times potential **customers** click on the ads determines the amount the advertiser pays to the host. Many advertisers prefer pay-per-click advertising because it enables them to pay only for people who actually read—and take some kind of action on—the advertising message.

pension

Benefits that an employee might receive after retirement. A pension is basically compensation received by the employee from the employer in order to provide for retirement. Employers often use retirement plans as a means to attract and keep good employees.

pension plan

A pension plan is a retirement plan set up by a company, labor **union**, government, or other organization for its employees. Examples include profit-sharing plans, **stock** bonus and employee stock ownership plans, thrift plans, target benefit plans, money purchase plans, and defined benefit plans. See also **SEP-IRA**, **SIMPLE IRA**

performance appraisal

A formal or informal way of letting an employee know what kind of job he or she is doing. Also known as performance review. Typically, performance appraisals are conducted on (at least) an annual basis, and the results of the evaluations are used as to determine the employee's rate of pay.

A performance review should evaluate whether an employee is performing the task he or she was originally hired to do, how well he or she performs that task or tasks, how well he or she gets along with coworkers, and finally his or her general attitude on the job. A performance appraisal offers an employer the chance to give helpful suggestions to his or her

An employee receives a performance appraisal.

employees about improvements that could be made if necessary. Employees should also be given the chance to offer comments and suggestions in return.

> **Performance appraisals are most effective when they identify specific, measurable targets for employees to work toward, and when they are part of a regular pattern of communication about on-the-job performance.**

point of sale (POS)

The physical location where **goods** are sold to **customers**. See also **retail**

partnership

One of several different types of structures for running a business. When two or more persons form a company that is not a **corporation**, it is a partnership. Any **debts** of the company are debts of the individual partners. One exception is a limited partnership, where the partners are not liable for any debts over and above the amount they invest in the partnership.

In most states, individuals or companies that form a partnership do not need a written **agreement** because most states have a statute known as the Uniform Partnership Act. This assumes that a partnership binds the parties unless they make another agree-

> The Uniform Partnership Act was established in 1914. Eighty years later the Reformed Uniform Partnership Act was approved, updating partnership laws to reflect modern business practices and trends.

ment in writing. Although partnerships are often informal and temporary, it is wise to draw up a written agreement because the Uniform Partnership Act may not reflect the terms of a verbal agreement between two parties. For example, let's say you start a business with a partner and agree to split the profits unequally—75 percent to you because you will do the majority of the work and 25 percent for your partner. After a year, business is booming and your partner suddenly wants more of the profit. You remind her of your agreement, but she lies and claims not to remember the terms. If the two of you go to court over the issue, your partner would win because the Uniform Partnership Act says that without a written agreement that states otherwise, a partnership shares profits and losses equally.

These women are partners in a café who meet regularly to discuss their business.

portfolio

A diversified grouping of **securities** (for instance, **stocks**, **bonds**, **treasury bills**, certificates of deposit, and/or other securities) held by a person or a fund for many **investors**. The idea behind a properly diversified portfolio is to limit **risk** by investing in many different areas at once. If stocks go down, for example, the other securities—such as bonds—may provide some protection. Similarly, certificates of deposit don't usually pay as much as stocks do (when stocks are going up)—but certificates of deposit are much, much safer. In a good portfolio, all the holdings are balanced to support the investor's goals and provide a degree of safety.

positioning

Earning **consumer** awareness of a product or **service** by associating it with something else that is already familiar to the consumer. For example, if you produce a certain **brand** of cereal, and use **advertising** to associate that cereal with a person consumers associate with health, fitness, and attractiveness, you are using positioning to establish your brand in the marketplace. Proper positioning of a product takes into consideration **price**, **promotion**, distribution, packaging, **competition**, the marketplace, etc.

power of attorney

A legal, signed document that gives another person, called the attorney, the authority to act on your behalf.

REAL LIFE: If your grandmother, for instance, is getting too old to go to the bank and pay her bills by herself, she might appoint and authorize another person as her "attorney

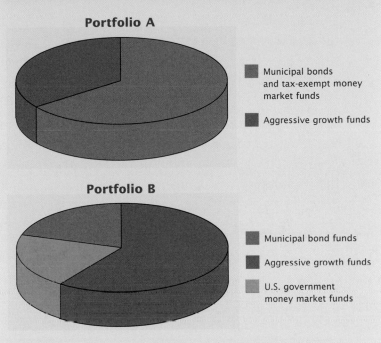

Portfolio Profiles of Two Investors

Portfolio A

- Municipal bonds and tax-exempt money market funds
- Aggressive growth funds

Portfolio B

- Municipal bond funds
- Aggressive growth funds
- U.S. government money market funds

Portfolio A features a degree of risk, and works for a young person with no children. **Portfolio B** features less risk and more stability to suit the needs of a middle-aged person.

in fact" to perform these acts for her. To do this, she has to sign a power of attorney to the other person.

preemptive right

A shareholder's right to obtain a certain number of shares in a future offering at current **prices** per share paid by new investors, whereby his/her percentage ownership remains the same as before the offering.

preferred stock

Stock that pays fixed **dividends** to preferred stockholders. Preferred stockholders always receive their dividends before common stockholders receive them, and if the company goes bankrupt, the preferred stockholders are paid first as well. Preferred stock takes precedence over **common stock** in the event of liquidation. Like common stock, preferred stock represents partial ownership in a company, although preferred stock shareholders do not enjoy the voting rights of common stockholders. Also unlike common stock, preferred stock pays a fixed **dividend** that does not go up or down, but the company does not have to pay this dividend if it cannot financially do so. The advantage to owning preferred stock is that the investor has superior rights to the company's **assets** than common stockholders. The four basic types of preferred stock are cumulative preferred, noncumulative, participating, and convertible.

press release

An announcement of a newsworthy event sent to the press to gain media coverage. It is informational in nature, such as the announcement of a new product, or the retirement of an executive, but it also serves as a **public relations** tool to keep the company's name in public view. Press releases tend to be most successful in drawing attention when they address an "angle," or topic, that a given journalist is already interested in. This is why targeted press releases tend to be the most successful.

REAL LIFE: If your business produces all-natural, organic ice cream, you might choose to target a press release to specific **consumers** you know are interested in subjects like environmental protection, business, and health. You might even decide to draft different versions of the release for different journalists.

price

The amount that a seller wants his **customer** to pay for his product. Pricing is an extremely important component of the **marketing mix**;

Product prices are advertised at a supermarket.

a seemingly minor change in a product's pricing can have a dramatic impact (positive or negative) on **sales**. (Think of all those advertisements for various products on television for products that happen to cost "only $19.95"; that particular price point has a demonstrated positive effect on stimulating consumer **demand** that a price of "only $20.00" doesn't match.)

price ceiling

The absolutely highest **price** that a product can be sold for. Sometimes **market** forces determine price ceilings, and sometimes government intervention determines them. For example, the government sets the absolutely highest **interest rate** credit card companies can charge their customers. See also **price floor**

price floor

The absolutely lowest price that a product can be sold for. See also **price ceiling**

product line

A group of products, often sold under one **brand** name, that are complementary or similar in nature.

A customer appears overwhelmed by the numerous choices available in a high-end cookware's product line.

> "If a window of opportunity appears, don't pull down the shade."
> —Tom Peters, business guru

profit and loss statement
(P&L statement)

A report showing a company's income, **expenses**, costs of doing business, and profit over a particular period of time. The P&L statement shows what is left (profit or losses) after all the **revenue** collected is added together and the **operating costs** are subtracted.

programmer

A person whose profession is to develop instructions for a computer in a particular programming language.

promotion

1. A specific **marketing** event, usually taking place at a predetermined time and place, where a product or **service** is advertised, and sometimes specially priced, to gain the attention and interest of **consumers**. A regional **retail** store might attract potential customers by having in-store signs or placing an advertisement in the local newspaper or radio for a promotion involving stereo equipment.
2. A job advancement to a higher level within the organization.

promotional pricing

Generally lower pricing associated with a **promotion**, and available to the customer only during a particular time.

prospecting

Developing new relationships with potential **customers**. Setting appointments by phone is an example of prospecting.

prototype

An original working model of a new product or invention. A prototype may be the first of many variations. Typically, prototypes (of products like computers, automobiles, or generators) are built at great **expense** in order to resolve engineering and production issues, and to serve as a model for later production.

psychographics

A **marketing** evaluation tool that highlights the psychological profiles of **consumers**.

public domain

When used in reference to writings, drawings, and other intellectual creations: material that is no longer or never was protected by **copyright** restrictions.

> Material developed by federal or state government bodies is not protected by copyright, and is therefore in the public domain. The term also describes works whose copyright protection has expired.

public relations

The activity of establishing and/or improving a person or company's public image. Public relations aim to influence a company's image in the media. Often, a public relations campaign will emphasize a company's philanthropic side. For example, if a company has made a charitable donation or even created its own foundation, the public relations team will be sure to make this information known to the public. See also **community relations** and **publicity**

> Businesses often spend thousands of dollars a year crafting a successful public relations campaign. Big companies will typically have their own public relations department, while smaller companies generally tend to hire outside consultants.

publicity

Strategic placement of items in the media that bring a person or a company into public prominence. Business almost always benefits from publicity—even negative publicity is often considered a good thing because it raises public awareness of a particular company's product or service. Most businesses use professional **public relations** experts to help create a positive message to relay to the media.

Prototypes are a way for car companies to test new features. Often prototypes are used in car races.

> "I love my clients...
> They're wonderful. I couldn't
> ask for a better clientele."
> — Anita Johnson-Jones

miracle nails

POTENT QUOTES

**HIGH POINTS OF
RUNNING THE BUSINESS:**

"I like to be able
to be my own boss—
set my own hours...
If I'm not busy,
I can go out and do
my own thing."

**LOW POINTS OF
RUNNING THE BUSINESS:**

"I just can't handle
any more (clients)!"

SAGE ADVICE:

Do what you really
love doing. "I've
been doing nails
since I was in
seventh grade, and
when I went to high
school, I started
doing acrylics. I
always liked changing
my nail color to
match what I was
wearing, and I
basically just kept
going with it."

Anita Johnson-Jones, a Fairmont, West Virginia, native attended beauty school when she graduated from high school. Soon she landed a job at the Finger-N-Toes nail salon. Anita spent over a year honing her skills there, and developed a dedicated clientele. Confident that she possessed the necessary traits—confidence and determination—to start her own business, Anita left Fingers-N-Toes in 1999.

With $2,000 of her own money, Anita was able to get a $3,000 loan from WesBanco. A microloan of $5,000 from the SBA Region VI Planning and Development Council soon followed. With a little more help from her brother-in-law, Anita was able to remodel a Laundromat into a beauty salon. When her own salon, Miracle Nail Techniques, opened, it became a huge success. In fact, the Small Business Development Center considers Miracle Nails one of its best success stories.

Anita plans to remain in the nail business for the next 20 years, and is hoping to move to a larger facility in Fairmont to accommodate more clients and also expand her services. Joining the Miracle team are her sister, Donnita Porter, to help her with the nail stenciling, and her friend Linda Pratt will bring a new service to the business—hair styling.

To find out more:
Call Anita at Miracle Nail Techniques (304) 366-9335

quality control

A concern with improving the quality of **goods** and **services**. Quality control helps ensure that a company does not produce faulty products. Companies use a variety of measures to achieve this goal, including the routine sampling and testing of all their products.

Quality control is essential in most businesses. In the food industry, products are carefully inspected before they are sold in stores.

quarterly report

A document required by the **Securities and Exchange Commission** (SEC) for all public companies in the United States, reporting the financial results for the quarter and noting any significant changes, events, **losses**, or gains in that quarter. Quarterly reports contain not only financial statements, but also a summary written by the **management**, and a list of important events that have taken place within the company (for example, a **stock** split or acquisition).

1st Quarter

If a company reports significant losses or gains in its quarterly report not only is its own stock likely to rise or fall accordingly, but a quarterly report from a large company can have a ripple effect on the entire stock market as well. Quarterly reports are published every three months.

quick ratio

An indicator of a company's financial strength (or weakness). A quick ratio is determined by taking current **assets** minus inventories, and dividing them by current **liabilities**. This ratio provides management information regarding the firm's **liquidity** and ability to meet its monetary obligations. Quick ratio is also called the acid test ratio.

A man stands on a mountain of mineral-rich earth. Minerals are an example of a raw material.

quick turn

The purchase and sale of an **investment** that is held for a very short period of time. Quick turning is a common practice in **day trading.**

quota

1. A portion, percentage, or limited amount.
2. The amount of **sales** set by a company needed to reach its sales goal.

rate

An amount that offers information about one quantity in terms of another quantity. A common type of rate is a quantity expressed in terms of time, such as percent change per year.

rate of exchange

The **rate** at which one currency can be converted into another. Generally, one unit of the home currency is expressed in terms of another currency. For example, an American bank may quote the exchange rate between the dollar and the Japanese yen as the number of dollars needed to buy one yen.

rate of return

The annual rate of return on an investment, expressed as a percentage of the total amount invested. Also called return.

raw materials

Unfinished **goods** consumed by a manufacturer in providing finished goods. Classified as inventory in the current **assets** section of a company's **balance sheet**.

REAL LIFE: Alice is a jewelry designer. Her business, Alice Design Studio, is dependent on the price and availability of raw materials like precious stones and metals.

A **real estate agent** shows a home to prospective buyers.

real estate

A piece of land, including the air above it, the ground below it, and any buildings or structures on it. For a business, buying real estate can be a risky venture. It is the most difficult **asset** to quickly turn to **cash**. With that in mind, there are certain times when real estate can become a more attractive proposition than others. If the **market** is unstable and **interest rates** are down, buying real estate can be a wise choice. However, if your business is at all unstable or you are experiencing any difficulty keeping up with your monthly bills, it's a good idea to hold off buying and continue renting.

rebate

1. A reduction in **price**, often used as part of a **promotion**: typically a **customer** purchases an item at the full **retail** price, and the manufacturer sends part of the price back to the customer.

2. For a bill of exchange, a discount that is offered if the bill is paid before the **debt** payment is due.

3. The amount of **interest** on short sale earnings that is paid to the borrower of a **bond** as motivation to borrow the **stock** from a specific source. When a short sale occurs, the seller often borrows a **security** through a lender, who in turn borrows the security from a bank or trust company. The short sale's earnings are returned to the lender, who then invests them and earns interest on them.

receipt

The proof of payment provided for **goods** or **services**.

receivables

Money due to a company for goods and services already sold. Typically, receivables are money owed to a company by **customers**, but they sometimes take the form of goods in a barter **exchange**. See also **payables**

recession

A period of general economic decline; business is slow, and people lose jobs. Technically speaking, six months or more of a decline in the gross domestic product.

record keeping

Keeping track of every detail in your business. By registering, filing, or writing down information about a transaction or event, you will be aware of how your business is running day-to-day, and where changes need to be made. If your

record keeping is accurate and up to date, you will also be in a far easier position if your business is ever audited by the IRS.

redeemable

Able to be redeemed before reaching maturity. The term usually refers to **bonds** and convertible **securities**. The issuer of a convertible security has to state the conditions under which the security may be called at the time of issue. For most securities, there is a certain initial time period in which the security cannot be redeemed. A bond can usually be redeemed when market **interest rates** fall below the **yield** being paid on the bond (bonds are usually called when the **price** rises to a certain point). To reflect this **risk**, a redeemable security is usually priced lower than a non-redeemable security.

refinancing

Paying off an existing loan with money from a new loan, typically for the same amount, and using the same property as **collateral**. When trying to decide whether this is worthwhile or not, the savings in interest should be compared to the fees involved with the refinancing process. The difficulty in figuring out this calculation is predicting how much the up-front money would be worth when the savings are received. If there are prepayment fees attached to the existing **mortgage**, refinancing is less appealing because of the increased cost to the borrower at the time of the refinancing.

REAL LIFE: Let's say you've built up significant equity over the years through appreciation of your home and principal reduction. You may want to refinance an existing mortgage for a larger loan amount, and use the additional funds for an investment, car, tuition, debt consolidation, etc. And, unlike any other type of consumer loan, the interest paid on the "cash out" could be 100 percent tax deductible.

A couple researches refinancing options.

refund

Money given back, often the purchase price of an item in the event of a **consumer**'s dissatisfaction. A **tax** refund occurs when a taxpayer pays more tax than he or she owes.

rent

Usually applied to land and buildings: the amount paid by the user, or tenant, to the owner for the use of the property for a certain period of time.

replacement cost

The amount it would cost to replace an **asset** at current prices. In **insurance** terms, the replacement costs means that the insurance company will cover lost, stolen, or destroyed property by paying the current **market** price, rather than a depreciated value of the **asset**.

retail

Sales offered directly to the **consumer**, or **end user**, of a product. Retail business can range dramatically from the smallest home-run business to huge **multinational** chain stores. Successful retail business owners pay close attention to the **customers'** needs by making sure to always have their best-selling products in stock and anticipating new trends. Becoming a small retail owner requires a true love for the work, however. The hours are long, and often store owners must go out of their way to serve the customer—

A consumer studies products at a supermarket.

particularly a reliable, regular one. Successful retailers are those who find a **niche** and make a simple visit to their store a positive experience for every person who walks through the door.

Many people interested in starting their own retail company feel hesitant

Since 1990, the Retail Systems/VICS Collaborative Commerce has hosted an annual trade show designed specifically for retailers, wholesalers, and suppliers. Each year at the show, the entire spectrum of the retail and supply chain industry gather together to share the latest in technology and business strategies.

because of competition from major chain stores. However, customers, often, prefer small stores because of the individual attention they receive. Customers may also choose a small business to support their fellow community members.

reserve

1. In lending, the reserve is the amount of money, subtracted from the value of the **collateral**.
2. Increases in the value of a company's **assets** that are reflected on its **balance sheet**.
3. Funds set aside for emergencies or other future needs.
4. In an auction, the minimum amount a seller is willing to sell at, known to the auction house but not the bidders.

reserve requirements

Since 1980, the **Federal Reserve** has required that all banks in the United States keep certain specified assets, or reserves, on hand or at a nearby Federal Reserve bank in order to support their deposits. The amount needed for the reserve requirement is specified as a percentage of total deposits. For example, let's say a bank's required reserve is 20 percent. If the bank receives a deposit of $100, it must hold on to $20 of the original deposit amount. Banks use the **interest** earned from loans and **investments** to make up the remaining $80. The reserve requirements help the Fed control lending and the nation's money supply.

residuals

1. Parts of **stock** returns not explained by the market-index return. They measure the impact of events that are specific to a certain company during a particular period.
2. Remainder **cash flows** generated by pool collateral and those needed to fund **bonds** supported by the collateral.

retail

See page 88

A retailer can sell anything from cars to toys. The nursery shown above is a retailer that specializes in plants and flowers.

retailer

A seller at the **retail** level. A retailer is any business that specializes in selling to **consumers**.

retirement

The period of a person's life during which time he or she is no longer working. Retirement also refers to the beginning of that period. No matter if you run a small home-run business or a large company, you should begin planning for retirement early—even if it means putting a only small amount of money aside every month. A financial planner can help you decide what the best retirement plan is for you, whether that be a traditional IRA or a **SEP-IRA**. If you plan to retire from a small business, it is a wise idea to select and train your successor in plenty of time before you actually retire from the company.

return on equity (ROE)

The amount of **net** income or profit on an **investor's** or business owner's total **equity**. The ROE signifies how an investment is doing and is a great indicator of a company's profitability. ROE is determined by dividing net income for the past 12 months by common stockholder equity. The result is shown as a percentage. Investors use ROE as a measure of how a company is using its money.

return on investment (ROI)

The amount an investor or business gets back in profit, expressed as a percentage of his or her initial **investment**.

revenue

1. The amount received from the sale of **goods** or **services**, not taking into consideration the costs of doing business.
2. The total amount of **taxes** taken in by a governing body.

Revenue received after a big sale.

revolving credit agreement

A legal commitment made by a bank with the promise to lend a **customer** up to a specified maximum amount during a specified period.

revolving line of credit

A bank line of **credit** on which the customer pays a commitment fee and in return can **draw** from and repay funds according to his or her needs. Normally, the line of credit requires a firm commitment from the bank for a period of several years.

risk

The likelihood of **loss** or less-than-expected **returns**. There are many different business-related types of risk, including currency risk, inflation risk, economic risk, **mortgage** risk, **liquidity** risk, **market** risk, opportunity risk, income risk, **interest rate** risk, credit risk, and business risk.

router

Either **software** or hardware or both that sends data packets on the **Internet** from one network to another. For example, if a request is sent from a computer in New York to companyX.com in Atlanta, the router first checks if the main network servers in the path directly to Atlanta are free. If not, the router checks alternative ones, and the packet may get to Atlanta via San Francisco as the most efficient route (that is, with fewer jumps). The router automatically checks for errors and quality of service in each transaction.

royalty

A form of payment acknowledging some right that the creator or author has in a certain property he or she created that is later sold. A royalty generally takes the form of a percentage of the **sales** of the item.

REAL LIFE: If you were to write a book, you, as the author, might negotiate an agreement with the publisher to receive a royalty, perhaps in the form of a percentage of the price of each book that is sold in bookstores.

S corporation

A form of **corporation**, allowed by the IRS for most companies with 75 or fewer shareholders. An S corporation enables the company to enjoy the benefits of incorporation but be taxed as if it were a partnership. S corporations are also usually run similarly to **partnerships**, but they have the advantage of limited **liability**. They are often family or small group businesses, where the **shares** are kept among the individual owners of the corporation and not sold publicly.

> An S corporation gets its name because it has special tax status under subchapter S of the Internal Revenue Code.

salary

A form of employee compensation that takes the form of a regular amount paid (sometime called **base** pay). Extra pay based on hours worked, performance, **commissions**, and **benefits** may be added. Salary is generally figured on an annual basis.

sales

The total dollar amount brought in for **goods** and **services** provided. While payment is not always necessary for recognition of sales on company financial statements, there are strict accounting guidelines stating what constitutes a sale. The basic principle is that a sale can be officially recognized only when the **transaction**

A customer examines a shirt in a menswear store. The salesperson assisting him will help make sure the sale is realized.

is already realized, or can be quite easily realized. This means that the company should have already received a payment, or know that the chance of receiving a payment soon is quite high. In addition, **delivery** of the good or service should have already taken place for the sale to be recognized.

A sales force member at a coffee shop where she is employed.

sales force

The people engaged in selling a company's product or **service** to returning and prospective **customers**. The main job of a **sales** force is to ensure a customer's satisfaction with **goods** and/or services. Also known as sales team.

sales forecast

A prediction of future sales over a given period.

sales management

The act of organizing, supporting, and motivating a **sales force**.

sales representative

A person who sells products or services who is either employed by a company or is an **independent contractor** agent of that company (and possibly others). Sales representatives are available to the purchaser to consult with on various business issues involving the purchase of products and services.

> A business owner must take the task of hiring sales representatives very seriously. These are the people who represent your company's product or service, and must therefore be well-informed and enthusiastic about the company. Sales representatives should understand and be prepared to answer with confidence all questions relating to the company's good or service. Ultimately, they can make or break a small, new business.

Sales tax is included in the final purchase price.

sales tax

A **tax**, usually imposed by state or municipal governments, on items purchased. The tax is generally a percentage added on to the amount of a **consumer**'s purchase price and collected by a merchant.

sample

A small amount of a product given for free to potential **customers**. Giving away free samples is an excellent way to lure customers into a store. Businesses ranging from bakeries to large cosmetics companies frequently make use of this tactic to draw in customers.

saturation

A stage in a product's life cycle in which everyone that might want the product already has it. If a company is in this stage, then it could indicate that the company is not innovative, or that competitors have been able to provide superior product offerings. Typically, the company will cut down on **sales** and **advertising** spending if it reaches this stage, and focus on the development of new products instead.

savings account

A type of bank account that generally pays **interest** to the depositor.

savings and loan

A federally or state-chartered financial institution that takes deposits from individuals, funds **mortgages**, and pays **dividends**.

scarcity

One factor in determining the value of a good. Usually, the value or **price** will go up if the item is difficult to come by—but only if there is a **demand** for that item.

search engine

A computer program that allows users to research and locate the topic of their choice on **Web sites**; or text, images, or data on the **Internet**, on a particular Web site, or within a single computer or **software** application. In other words, you are using a search engine whenever you use the Find button at a portal. The major search engines used are Yahoo.com, Google.com, and Lycos.com. If a company creates a Web site, one of the most important steps is registering it with all search engines. Being accessible and easy for online customers to find provides companies with a major benefit. See also **search engine placement**

search engine placement

The act of ensuring prominent placement for a given Web site on one or more of the commonly used **search engines**. There is usually a **fee** for this **service**.

> "The trees that are slow to grow bear the best fruit."
>
> —Molière, 17th-century playwright

93

> "To run a company, you have to feel that, for better or for worse, you have a lot of faith in the decisions that you make."
>
> — Josh Newman

independent filmmaker

Sharkbyte Software is a database software company that Josh Newman founded at age 18 with a partner (a fellow college student who was just three years older). The business was a fairly simple one to begin because it required no outside start-up funds, and the founders began it as a consulting business—making proposals to businesses they felt they could help. Then, after having won assignments, they hired the personnel they needed to deliver what they'd just promised. "We were running the show," he recalls, "even though a lot of our employees could have been our parents." Money was not the primary motivator for starting the business, Josh says. "We were just really excited about what was happening with the Internet and with computers."

Josh has switched gears a bit since then, and is currently CEO of Cyan Pictures, an independent film studio. He is a founder and board member of the National Student Entrepreneurship Forum. Josh has sold Sharkbyte, his first successful start-up, in order to completely devote himself to his new business.

To find out more:
Log on to www.self-aggrandizement.com/joshua.html

POTENT QUOTES

HIGH POINTS OF RUNNING THE BUSINESS:

"At Sharkbyte...we were having a good time doing what we were doing. The fact that we made money in the process was a pleasant side-effect of it all."

LOW POINTS OF RUNNING THE BUSINESS:

"The business caused me to miss out on sleep, but that was about all I missed..."

SAGE ADVICE:

"Pick something you love to build a business around. Unless you wake up every morning excited...you just aren't going to be able to make it all the way through."

secondary market

A **market** in which an **investor** purchases a **security** from another investor rather than the issuer, subsequent to the original issuance in the primary market.

secure site

A **Web site** where **consumers** may safely place confidential information, such as **credit** card numbers. Secure sites use encryption (coding) to translate the information and keep the information safe for the **customers**, the merchants, and the banks. The credit card information given by the consumer is decoded upon receipt by the merchant.

securities

Financial instruments including **stock** certificates, **bonds**, or other papers indicating a loan to a company or an **interest** in (that is, a right to **share** in the profits of) a company. See also **stocks**, **shares**, **bonds**

> In 1933 Congress passed the Securities Act. Its purpose was to require that investors receive all important information regarding securities that were offered for public sale. It was also passed to prevent deceit, misrepresentations and other fraud in the sale of securities. The following year, the Securities and Exchange Commission was founded to enforce the Securities Act of 1933.

Securities and Exchange Commission

See page 97

security

1. **Collateral**; something of value given to a **creditor** to ensure that the loan will ultimately be paid back.
2. A company's commitment to the safety of customers and employees. In **e-commerce** this is especially essential. Customers need a promise of safety and privacy before providing individual financial information over the **Internet**.

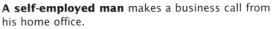

A self-employed man makes a business call from his home office.

self-employment

The act of working for yourself while serving others. Working for oneself provides a certain amount of freedom and flexibility, but it is crucial to keep in mind that it is also hard work. Essential qualities needed to make self-employment a successful endeavor include persistence, confidence, excitement, flexibility, and the determination to keep it all going.

SEP-IRA (Simplified Employee Pension IRA)

The SEP-IRA is a good plan for self-employed entrepreneurs with a small number of employees. Both employers and employees are able to contribute up to 5 percent of their annual salary as long as it isn't more than approximately $30,000. Contributions made by employers need to be proportionate to contributions made by employees. The contributions are **tax** deductible as a business expense.

servers

Computers or workstations on a network that handle requests from other computers or clients, serving them stored data and files or processing power. Specific types of servers include Web servers, mail servers, and file servers. On a local area network (LAN), servers can serve as gatekeepers, controlling access to the network, and resource distributors, storing files centrally and providing access to network resources (files, printers, disk drives, modems) to PCs functioning as workstations.

service

Usually, the performance of a task for which someone receives payment.

service business

A kind of business that relies on performing some task for another person. Massage therapists, bookkeepers, baby-sitters, dog walkers, personal shoppers, and house painters are all examples of service businesses. It is often easier for a person to get a service-oriented business started because they generally take less **capital** to get off the ground than a product-related business. Service businesses often rely on word-of-mouth recommendations.

service mark

A registered logo or **brand** name that is used to identify a **service**. See also **trademark**

A tailor performs a service for his customer.

Securities and Exchange Commission

The main government regulatory agency for the **securities** industry. Its responsibility is to protect investors against fraudulent and manipulative practices and to maintain a level of integrity in the securities markets. As more and more first-time investors try their hand at investing in the **stock** markets to help secure their futures, pay for homes, and send children to college, these goals are more important than ever. The SEC also oversees other key participants in the securities world, including stock exchanges, broker-dealers, **investment** advisors, **mutual funds**, and public utility holding companies.

Franklin D. Roosevelt

The Securities and Exchange Commission is comprised of five commissioners, who are appointed by the president, four divisions, and eighteen offices. The five commissioners are appointed for five-year terms that are staggered so that one new commissioner is replaced every year. With approximately 3,100 staff, the SEC is small in comparison to other federal agencies. The SEC is headquartered in Washington, D.C., with 11 additional regional and district offices throughout the country. The Securities and Exchange Commission is an independent, semi-judiciary agency. Its four divisions are:

> After the stock market crashed in October 1929, the fortunes of countless investors vanished, banks lost great sums of money, and investors feared both investing in the market and keeping their money in a bank. Public confidence in the markets plummeted. Under the administration of President Roosevelt, the SEC was founded in 1934 to help restore the people's faith in the stock market and banks.

the Division of Corporate Finance, the Division of Market Regulation, the Division of Investment Management, and the Division of Enforcement.

software

Programs that give computers (hardware) specific instructions on what to do. Software programs can consist of hundreds of thousands or even millions of lines of instructions that the microprocessor and other computing components carry out. Application software (apps) is the term for the programs that the user operates for a particular purpose. Some software such as Adobe Acrobat (needed for reading PDF files) may be downloaded for free from the **Internet**, while other industry-specific software can be quite expensive.

There are many kinds of software out there that are essential to a business: financial software to help keep track of **accounting** records; **word-processing** software for composing letters and other documents; presentation software; graphics and publishing software for creating **marketing** materials; computer-aided design software used by designers and architects; **database** software to manage information; spreadsheets to manage budgets and make **forecasts**; and many, many other applications.

> WordStar was an important early word-processing software release; it was first developed in 1979. It has since fallen by the wayside. Over the course of the past two decades, Microsoft has emerged as the dominant player in the field of software. Most businesses are dependent on Microsoft products. Microsoft Office, probably the most commonly used of all of Microsoft's software, combines many applications, including Word, Excel, and Microsoft Internet Explorer. There are other versions of business software available, but in order to be compatible with the majority of the business world, it is essential to stick with Microsoft.

share

Stock in a **corporation**. Often the owners of a corporation own shares of stock in the company. The shares come in the form of stock certificates and are reflected in the company's records. It can be a tricky and risky business offering shares of stock to all employees who help found the business, because once an individual becomes a stockholder, the only way to reclaim the shares is to buy back the stock. See also **stock**

short sale

Borrowing a **security** from a **broker** and selling it, with the understanding that it must be bought back at a later date (hopefully at a lower **price**) and returned to the broker. Short selling (or "selling short") is a technique used by investors who try to profit from the falling price of a stock. For example, imagine an **investor** who wants to sell short 100 shares of a company, believing that its stock is overpriced and will correct itself soon. The investor's broker will borrow the shares from someone who owns them with the promise that the investor will return them later. The investor immediately sells the borrowed shares at the current market price. If the price of the shares drops, he or she "covers the short position" by buying back the shares at the lower price, and his or her broker returns them to the lender. The profit is the difference between the price at which the stock was sold and the cost to buy it back, minus commissions and expenses for borrowing the stock in the first place. Trouble occurs, however, if the price of the shares increases rather than falls; the potential **losses** are unlimited. The company's shares may go up and up, but at some point the investor has to replace the 100 shares he or she sold. In that case, the losses can mount until the short position is covered. Gamblers love this technique because short selling is a very risky prospect.

short-term notes

Generally **debts** that are due within one year or less. Short-term notes can also be an **investment** for a term of one year or less.

silent partner

A business partner who provides **capital** but does not actively participate in the **management** of operations.

A silent partner signs a contract that outlines the terms of the partnership.

SIMPLE IRA (Savings Incentive Match Plan for Employees IRA)

The SIMPLE IRA is a good plan for employers with up to 100 employees. The employer is obligated to give a 2 or 3 percent match. SIMPLE IRA accounts are fairly easy to set up and do not need to be reported to the **Internal Revenue Service**. Once a year the employer must report his or her contributions to employees.

software

See page 98

sole proprietorship

A type of business organization that is neither a **partnership** nor a **corporation**. The sole proprietor (sole owner) has no **liability** protection, which means that he or she can be held personally responsible for any harm or injury experienced by others related to the business. Sole proprietorships are easy to start and operate, but they also hold some disadvantages. The first is that the sole proprietor is the only person held liable. The second drawback is that rather than paying a (generally lower) corporation or business **tax**, the sole proprietor must pay the same percentage for his or her business as he or she would for personal **income tax**.

spam

An unsolicited **e-mail marketing** message. The facetious term for junk e-mail that lands on millions of people's computers every day. The term "spam" is either used as a noun for junk mail or as a verb, as in to "spam" people with a load of junk mail.

specialty retailer

A **retailer** who sells only a certain, narrow **product line** (such as bagels, printer accessories, or hardware). A specialty retailer will usually stock **merchandise** for a particular type of **customer**, and will have an in-depth selection of the type of merchandise he or she sells. See also **niche market**

A specialty retailer measures candy for a customer. She specializes in stocking and selling only different varieties of candy in her store.

spreadsheet

A **software** tool for keeping track of various figures, formulas, and values, all arranged in columns and rows. In a spreadsheet's display, the numbers can be made to relate to one another so that a change in one part of the program can affect many different numbers. (For instance, revising a **sales** estimate can automatically revise a **revenue** estimate elsewhere in the spreadsheet.) Spreadsheets are important tools in the development of budgets, **balance sheets**, and other business-related documents. Most businesses today use computer spreadsheets for a variety of planning and analyzing activities; the most popular current spreadsheets are Microsoft Excel and Lotus 123. See also **software**

> The first commercially successful spreadsheet software was VisiCalc, released in 1982 and written for the Apple II.

	67,000	137,000	13,5
	70,000	140,000	13,5
	41,778	89,678	13,5
	76,551	117,451	13,5
	71,737	74,637	13,5
	75,500	70,400	13,5
	43,115	84,015	13,5
	61,991	104,891	13,5
	28,877	61,777	13,5

start-up costs

The amount of money spent (or needed) to start a business. Start-up costs may involve **expenses** like **rent**, purchase of **manufacturing** materials or products, labor, and **overhead** for a certain period of time.

stock

1. The certificate(s) indicating an **investor**'s ownership of **shares** in a **corporation**. See also **common stock**, **preferred stock**

2. Another name for a business's **inventory** of product for sale.

supplier

A company from which a business buys critical resources needed for manufacturing, selling at the **retail** level, or day-to-day operation of the company. Many suppliers are **wholesalers**. It's a good idea to to work with a few different suppliers. That way, if one goes bankrupt or experiences a supply shortage, you can turn to another source for help.

> It is crucial for any business owner to have more than one supplier on hand in case of emergency. If a company is dependent on only one supplier for a crucial product necessary for the success of its business, unexpected problems with the supplier could prove disastrous. Another advantage of having more than one supplier is the potential for negotiation.

supply and demand

See **law of supply and demand**

survey

1. An attempt to determine popular attitudes about (for instance) a certain product or **service** offered by a company, or to find out how satisfied **customers** are with their relationship with a company.

2. The scientific measurement of land conducted for legal purposes.

T

take-home pay

The pay actually received by an employee after adding bonuses and deducting **taxes**, health care premiums, and **retirement** savings plans.

takeover

See **acquisitions**

target market

See **market targeting**

tariff

A duty (a type of tax) added to the **price** of a product when it is imported into a country. Tariffs are imposed to protect domestic industries from international **competition** and also to raise **revenue** for the government.

tax

Money contributions for the support of local, state, or federal government. These aren't voluntary; businesses are subject to taxation on a number of fronts. Evasion of lawful tax obligations is a criminal activity.

If you run your own business, the following are few tax tips to keep in mind. Keep your checkbook balanced for the year and prepare an annual financial report including profits and losses. Organize your business checks into the same categories you use in your bookkeeping system. Because entertainment and dining expenses are only 50 percent deductible, it's wise to separate those **receipts** from the rest. Also keep aside receipts for major office equipment or other large expense items because they are fully deductible up to $24,000. Hold on to any receipts for donations to charities or society membership, fees such as the World Wildlife Fund. Call an **accountant** or financial advisor early in the tax season to help with this year's taxes and to strategize for the next year.

> "Nothing great was ever achieved without enthusiasm."
> —Ralph Waldo Emerson, poet

A **skilled telemarketer** conducts company sales over the phone.

telemarketing

The act of **marketing** products and **services** by telephone. If the sale does not close over the phone, then the **sales** activity in question is not telemarketing. There are advantages and disadvantages to telemarketing. Skilled, knowledgeable internal telemarketers are generally considered an **asset** to any business. Aggressive, uninformed telemarketers can be a hindrance to a company.

test market

A way for companies to test a product's success through **consumer** response before spending money on full-scale production. Test groups are usually comprised of a fairly large number of consumers within a limited area.

tick

1. The smallest possible movement (up or down) in the **price** of a **security**. A tick is also referred to as minimum fluctuation.
2. An upward (uptick) or downward (downtick) movement in a security's price.

till money

The money held on hand by **commercial banks** to meet their **reserve requirements** and the day-to-day demands of their **customers**.

title

Legal ownership of something. The word "title" can refer to ownership of personal property, such as a vehicle, or to real property, as demonstrated by a **deed**.

A **will legally outlines** the distribution of the personal possessions (money, title to property, etc.) of a deceased person.

tracking stock

Publicly traded securities issued by a company to monitor the **earnings** potential and/or underlying performance of a subsidiary, a smaller branch of the large company. Tracking stock is an increasingly popular device that enables the parent company to maintain control over the subsidiary while permitting **investors** to value the tracked unit as a separate entity.

trade

1. The buying or selling of a security or **commodity**.
2. The exchange of products and/or **services** without the use of money. This is also called barter.

trade association

A group of similar businesses that join together to create a network. It is a smart idea for all business owners to join a trade organization. There are literally thousands of different industries—ranging from bookstore owners to organic farmers—that have their own trade association. Joining an organization is a wonderful opportunity to learn from others in your trade, check out **competition**, and create helpful business contacts.

trade credit

This refers to a firm's ability to buy supplies or services on a **credit** basis, based on its previous record of timely payment. When a firm buys from **suppliers** on a regular basis, and pays its bills on time, it establishes credit with those suppliers. This credit can be an important form of **financing**, and an alternative to traditional financing methods, like banks. Trade credit is generally more costly to a purchaser than bank financing, but if it is all that is available, it can be an important option.

A trader on the floor of an exchange. He uses hand gestures to indicate how many shares of stock and at what price he is willing to buy or sell them.

top line

The total **revenue** of a company, before any **deductions** are made for any costs, **taxes**, and other charges.

total assets

The total combined amount of all current and long-term **assets** owned by an individual or company, including **real estate**, investment **securities**, trading accounts, **cash**, money market investments, and other owned assets.

total costs

1. In **accounting**, total costs are the amount of **fixed costs**, **variable costs**, and semi-variable costs added together.
2. In the context of investments, total costs include the total amount of money spent on a particular investment, including the **price** of the investment itself, plus **brokers' commissions**, **fees**, other miscellaneous transaction costs, and taxes.

trademark

The formal registration and legal protection of a branded product to distinguish it from similar **goods**. A trademark is usually indicated by a symbol, word, identifying logo, **brand** name, or any combination thereof. A particular color can even be trademarked if it is distinct and generally associated by the public with a particular product. Once a trademark is registered, it may not be legally used by others. It costs $350 for a basic application to register a trademark with the U.S. Patent and Trademark Office. See also **service mark**

REAL LIFE: If Lucy of company ABC wishes to register a trademark, she must first search the U.S. Patent and Trademark database to make sure that her trademark is not the same as or too similar to another company's trademark. Because determining whether or not a particular trademark is too similar to another in the public mind can be difficult, it would be wise for Lucy to consult an attorney who specializes in trademark law before registering her own trademark. Infringement lawsuits can be long, arduous, and expensive.

Two men use equipment to record Leo, the lion, for the Metro-Goldwyn-Mayer trademark in 1928. Leo and his famous roar are still seen and heard at the beginning of MGM movies seventy-five years later.

A retailer at a trade show demonstrates his product's uses and attributes.

trademark
See page 105

trade name
A legal name that is used for business that is not necessarily the name that appears on your birth certificate. For example, if your name is Jane Smith and you run a bakery/café called Jane's Bakery and Café, you are using a trade name. Most states require that businesses using a trade name must register a trade name certificate with the state.

trade show
An exhibition, generally for companies engaged in a particular trade (anything ranging from the makers of shoes to technological products). All the companies that want to sell to the group in question come to the show to display what products and **services** are available. Prospective **customers** can come to one location and walk around viewing each of the exhibitors' wares.

> **Trade shows are usually held in large exhibition centers; the companies that want to exhibit their products and services rent space (booths) from which to display the product. Although much shopping is conducted online these days, nothing replaces the experience of viewing, touching, or tasting a product in person.**

transaction

1. An **agreement** between a buyer and a seller to exchange an **asset** for payment.

2. In **accounting**, any event or condition no matter how minute, that is recorded in the accounting books.

treasury bill

A U.S. financial **security** issued by the **Federal Reserve** banks to the United States Treasury. Treasury bills are negotiable debt obligations and backed by the government's full faith and credit. They typically have a maturity of one year or less, and are exempt from state and local **taxes**. The government uses treasury bills to regulate the country's money supply. Treasury bills are also called bills or T-bills, or U.S. Treasury bill.

turnaround expert

A consultant who is hired, usually for a high fee, by a company to save the business. A turnaround expert typically negotiates payment plans with **creditors** and **suppliers** for the company. Often he or she fires the current staff and recruits new employees.

turnkey

A method of setting up a business, as in franchising, where the franchiser (the master company) provides a location, all the necessary supplies, all the training resources, and everything else necessary to immediately begin business. A good example of a turnkey operation would be a fast-food restaurant. The term "turnkey" can also be used in situations other than franchises where a business subcontracts most of its work to others. This might occur, for instance, if a subcontractor can produce products or parts more economically than the manufacturer, and the manufacturer concludes that it is cheaper to buy the components than to make them from scratch.

> The term "turnkey operation" is derived from the idea that the proprietor of a franchise can simply turn the key, enter the premises, and be in business. This is actually something of an oversimplification, but it gets the idea of standardization across.

turnover

For a company, the ratio of **sales** to **inventory** for a year, or for the fraction of a year that an average item remains in inventory. Low turnover is a sign of inefficiency within the company, since inventory usually has a rate of return of zero. Turnover, in terms of a **mutual fund**, means the number of times per year that an average dollar of assets is reinvested.

A fast-food franchise is a common type of turnkey business.

underwriters

Investment bankers who buy shares of a company that is going public, then resell them to individuals and companies.

unearned income

An individual's income earned from means other than employment, such as **interest** and **dividends** from investments, or income from rental property. Unearned income is also called unearned revenue.

Unemployment Rate

Unemployment (percent) / **Year**

20
18
16
14
12
10
8
6
4
2
0

1950 1960 1970 1980 1990 1998

Teenagers

Minorities

Total
U.S. Labor
Force

unemployment insurance

Insurance benefits paid to laid-off workers by the state. Unemployment insurance typically lasts up to six months and is a percentage of the worker's previous salary. In order to be covered by unemployment insurance, the laid-off worker must be ready, willing, and able to work. If an employee applies for an extension to his or her unemployment coverage, he or she must be able to prove that he or she has been looking for a new job.

All business owners are required to contribute part of their payroll taxes to a state-sponsored unemployment fund that provides laid-off workers with their unemployment insurance checks. Employers' contributions are based on how many current employees they have and how many employees have collected unemployment checks in the previous years. Unemployment insurance benefits vary from state to state.

unemployment rate

Percentage of the labor force that is unemployed.

uniform resource locator (URL)

The digital address that leads a person surfing the **Internet** to a specific place on the Web. URLs typically begin the address with www.

Union workers come together holding signs of protest in a strike.

union

A group of organized workers who pay dues to a central office that in turn represents and supports them in workers' rights issues and workplace disagreements. Unions can range from workers in the industrial and shipping fields to actors and writers.

unrealized loss

See **paper loss**

unrealized profit

See **paper profit**

upgrade

A positive change in ratings for a **security**. Two common examples of upgrading are a financial analyst's upgrading of a **stock** (such as from "sell" to "buy") and a **credit** bureau's upgrading of a **bond**.

upselling

Selling an existing **customer** additional products or **services**; also, selling a new customer, in addition to product(s) he or she has already selected, items he or she hadn't originally considered buying. Upselling is a popular strategy for improving a company's overall profitability by getting the customer to buy more.

utility

A basic service such as electricity, gas, or water, or the company that provides such a service. Utilities are often regulated by the government. Utility also refers to the measure of satisfaction derived by an **investor** or person.

"I can remember
my mother making the
best salsa."

— Linda Torres-Winters

Lindita's salsa success

Linda was the fifth child in a family of nine. Her father was a Spanish immigrant and her mother a North American Indian. Growing up in a migrant farm working family, Linda traveled from Texas to the Midwest harvesting seasonal crops. When Linda was 16, her father became disabled in a work accident. To help support her family, Linda left school to work two jobs. One year later Linda earned her high school diploma from the High School Equivalency Program (HEP) and became the first and only person in her family to attend college.

While Linda attended the University of Wisconsin Milwaukee, she worked for HEP, traveling to migrant farm worker camps, and recruiting teens into the HEP program. In 1995 Linda formed Linditas' Inc., a food manufacturing company which produces Linditas' Instant Salsa Mixes. The salsa is distributed to more than 500 stores in eight states.

Linda was Denver's Hispanic Business Women of the Year in 1997. She has served as a director on many boards including The Denver Hispanic Chamber of Commerce and Mi Casa Resources for Women. Linda is also a member of the Colorado Food Association and was nominated by Merrill Lynch for the 1999 Ernst & Young Entrepreneur of The Year and by Mi Casa Resource Center for the 2001 Small Business of The Year. In 2002 Linda launched Lindita's Cooking-Show, showcasing traditional Mexican dishes.

To find out more: Visit www.linditassalsa.com

POTENT QUOTES

**HIGH POINTS OF
RUNNING THE BUSINESS:**
Being able to make a contribution to her family: "I always wanted to do something for my family—to be somebody."

**LOW POINTS OF
RUNNING THE BUSINESS:**
Memories of economic challenges during her childhood. "We lived in one big room, side by side..."

SAGE ADVICE:
Look to your own heritage and traditions for business ideas. "Growing up as a migrant farm worker, I picked tomatoes as a child. I had the opportunity to create an authentic salsa based on my Hispanic culture and heritage."

valuation

The process of determining the total perceived worth of a company's **assets** or **stock**. There are many different techniques for valuation, and most are often partially objective and partially subjective. Therefore, when looking for a professional to provide an examination of your total worth, it's important to hire someone who is familiar with your particular industry.

During the dot-com boom, company valuations skyrocketed to previously unheard-of highs only to come plummeting down following the stock market crash in the spring of 2001. Companies that were valued at millions or even hundreds of millions of dollars were suddenly worthless.

variable cost

A cost of doing business that depends on the **price** changes of labor or supplies. For example, let's say the cost of a necessary component of what you are **manufacturing** goes up; that price increase will affect the cost of your product. You may choose to raise prices in an attempt to maintain your profit margin, but this is a complicated decision, since price increases may have a negative effect on your total **sales**. See also **fixed cost**

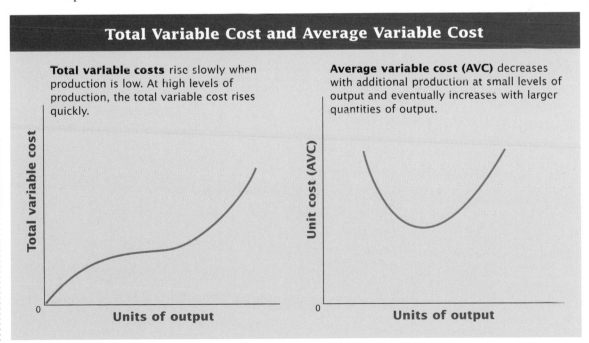

Total Variable Cost and Average Variable Cost

Total variable costs rise slowly when production is low. At high levels of production, the total variable cost rises quickly.

Total variable cost vs. *Units of output*

Average variable cost (AVC) decreases with additional production at small levels of output and eventually increases with larger quantities of output.

Unit cost (AVC) vs. *Units of output*

value-added

The enhancement added to a product or **service** by a company before the product is offered to **customers**.

variance

In **accounting**, it is the difference between the budgeted and actual cost or, in other words between the planned and actual cost for direct material, labor, and **overhead**.

vendors

Companies or individuals who sell you the **goods** and services necessary to run your business. Because vendors are crucial to the **manufacturing** process, it is important to maintain a good, respectful relationship with them. Meet with them in person and keep in touch in between orders. See also **suppliers**

venture

A business undertaking. The term usually refers to a situation where several people or entities come together to buy or sell something or to make a business **investment**. The term "joint venture" often refers to a venture in which no independent company, **partnership**, or **corporation** is formed.

venture capital

Money supplied to support a business initiative, usually with the understanding that both the potential risk (**loss** of the money) and the potential benefit (the **return on investment**) may be significant. Typically, though, venture capital is funds made available for start-up firms and small businesses with exceptional growth potential. Managerial and technical expertise are often also provided. Those who

This customer buys the supplies she needs for her own business from a vendor that specializes in thread and sewing supplies.

The founder of a new company meets with a venture capitalist to get funding for the business.

supply **investment** money in such situations are known as venture capitalists. This kind of start-up financing is often used to finance technology companies.

vertical acquisition

An **acquisition** in which the acquiring company and the target company are in the same industry but focus on different parts of the production process.

REAL LIFE: The recent acquisition of Emagic (makers of the software Logic Audio) by the Apple computer company is an example of a vertical acquisition because Apple and Emagic each play a different role in the production process of software designed for Apple computers.

vertical market

A **market** that meets the needs of a particular industry: for example, a piece of equipment used only by semiconductor manufacturers.

vesting

An ERISA (Employee Retirement Income Security Act of 1974) guideline that states that employees must be entitled to their **benefits** from a pension fund, profit-sharing plan, or employee **stock** ownership plan within a certain

period of time, even if they no longer work for their employer. A gradual vesting plan usually means that employees receive a percentage of stock or other type of benefit with each year of service. This typically breaks down to 25 percent a year for four years.

A chef typically receives formal training and on-the-job experience in preparation for his vocation.

vocation

Profession or career, from chef to banker.

volatility

The relative rate at which the price of a **security** moves up and down. Volatility is found by calculating the annualized standard deviation of daily change in **price**. If the price of a stock moves up and down rapidly over short time periods, it has high volatility. If the price almost never changes, it has low volatility.

A **garden supply store owner** may buy more tools than necessary in order to receive a volume discount.

volume

The total amount of something. The term may refer to the total **sales** generated by a company in a given period. Volume is often a factor in pricing; a company can sell fewer items (less volume) at a higher profit margin, or a lot of items (more volume) at a smaller profit margin, and come out with the same amount of total profit. Volume also refers to the number of **shares**, **bonds**, or **contracts** traded during a given period, for a **security** or an entire **exchange**. This type of volume is also known as trading volume.

volume discount

Reduction in price offered or given for larger-than-average purchases.

REAL LIFE: Sarah opens Johnson's Nursery and Garden Supply store. She wants to sell both plants and the tools people use to tend their gardens. She must buy not only plants from farmers, but also the gardening tools. Rather than buy only a few rakes, shovels, and trowels at a time, she might buy many more items than she keeps on display in order to receive a volume discount from her distributor. She may even offer her own volume discount to **customers** who want to buy large quantities of certain plants or gardening tools, in order to entice more spending at her store and to show customer appreciation.

voting right

The right of a **common stock** shareholder to vote, in person or by proxy, for members of the board of directors and other matters of corporate policy, such as the issuance of senior securities, stock splits, and substantial changes in operations.

W-Z

Wall Street

Name for the financial district in New York City, and the street where the **New York Stock Exchange**, **American Stock Exchange**, and many banks and brokerages are located. Wall Street is also used as a generic term for firms that buy, sell, and underwrite **securities**, or as a reference to the **investment** community in general.

> In March 1792, twenty four of New York City's leading merchants met secretly to discuss ways to bring order to the securities business and to steal it from their competitors, the auctioneers. Two months later, on May 17, 1792, these merchants signed a document known as the Buttonwood Agreement, named after their traditional meeting place, a buttonwood tree. The agreement called for the signers to trade securities only among themselves, to set trading fees, and not to participate in other auctions of securities. These twenty four men founded what was to eventually become the New York Stock Exchange. The New York Stock Exchange would later be located at 11 Wall Street.

wares

Products, **merchandise**, **commodities**, supplies, **goods** for sale.

Businessmen stand in front of the New York Stock Exchange on Wall Street.

warrant

A certificate, usually issued along with a **bond** or **preferred stock**, entitling the holder to buy a specific amount of securities at a specific

warranty

A **guarantee** made by a company regarding its product's future performance. A warranty provides a **customer** with a promise that a product will continue to work for a certain period of time and describes in detail the conditions under which the warranty does not apply. For example, if a company warns that a camera is "not for underwater use," and a consumer takes it into the ocean, breaking the camera in the process, the company is under no obligation to replace the camera or reimburse the customer.

> A typical warranty has four parts: a promise that the product will last, a time period that it should last, a disclaimer that outlines a situation in which the warranty does not apply, and rule about what the company and the customer must do in order for the warranty to be realized.

Some warranties are implied, while others are express. Warranties that are written or granted verbally are express. Implied warranties are implied under the law known as Article 2 of the Uniform Commercial Code determined by each state. The Uniform Commercial Code states that all goods and services fall under two implied warranties: (1) that the **good** or **service** is something that can actually be sold commercially, and (2) that the good or service is in the condition the seller has advertised to the **consumer**.

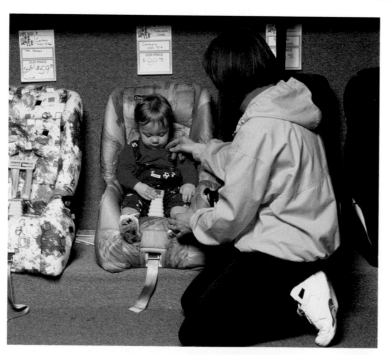

A mother shops for a car seat. The manufacturers provide a warranty that says their product will work when used properly.

price, usually above the current **market** price at the time of issuance, for an extended period, anywhere from a few years to forever. If the price of the security rises above that of the warrant's exercise price, then the investor can buy the security at the warrant's exercise price and resell it for a profit. Otherwise, the warrant will simply expire or remain unused. Warrants are listed on options exchanges and trade independently of the security with which it was issued.

warranty

See page 116

Web marketplace

An electronic marketplace in which **goods**, **services**, and financial instruments are traded. **Exchanges** in a marketplace of some kind have been made for thousands of years, but have recently found new vitality on the **Internet** by connecting individual and large communities of buyers and sellers. Web marketplaces can be worldwide and operate round the clock. Such exchanges have the unique advantage of exposing true cost, value, and **price** and tend to eliminate the waste and inefficiencies common in some traditional types of marketplaces. The resulting savings earned from these markets can be shared among buyers, sellers, and exchanges.

Web marketplace models range from auctions of all different types to the new Automotive Network Exchange (ANX) Web site, which is expected to link the North American auto supply chain. Electronic **stock** and **bond** exchanges have grown so popular that they are challenging the **NASDAQ** and **New York Stock Exchange**.

Web site

A World Wide Web destination containing some display of information and/or pictures; part of the Internet. Today, most companies have Web sites that describe (among other things) their operations, history, products, and services, and offer a way of contacting the company directly.

white knight

A friendly potential bidder who voluntarily steps in or is sought out by a target company to take over the company to avoid a hostile takeover by an undesirable suitor.

Wholesale precious gems like diamonds are sold to jewelry designers and stores, who in turn, use the diamonds to make and sell jewelry.

wholesale

A means of buying or **manufacturing** goods in large quantities, at a relatively low price. Wholesalers sell goods to distributors at significantly lower prices; distributors in turn sell to full-service or self-service **retail** outlets. The **retailers** sell the goods in smaller quantities at a higher price. The difference between wholesale price levels and retail price levels can vary by industry, but it is likely to be around 40 to 50 percent, figured on the retail price.

worker's compensation insurance

A system of **insurance** controlled by each state in which money is paid to persons injured while at work—in return for the worker giving up the right to sue his/her employer. This kind of insurance basically does away with the concept of fault for a worker's injury for those who participate in the program. Amounts of compensation are based on the extent of each individual worker's injuries.

working capital

Current **assets** minus current liabilities. Working capital is the amount of money a company has available at a given time to conduct the affairs of the business. Basically, this is the amount of **cash** on hand, accounts receivable, and other current assets that finance the day-to-day operations of a company. A company's working capital can be positive or negative, depending on how much **debt** the company is carrying. In general, companies that have a lot of working capital will be more successful since they can expand and improve their operations. Companies with negative working capital may lack the funds necessary for growth.

If a worker is injured on the job, he or she is covered by worker's compensation insurance.

wholesaler

A person or group in the business of buying large quantities of **goods**, at high volume, and reselling smaller quantities of those goods to **jobbers** and **retailers** at a higher price.

word processing

A kind of computer **software** application used to produce printed written documents. Unlike typewriters, word processors allow you to change parts of the document (for instance, to rearrange paragraphs) without having to retype the entire document. Today, popular word processing programs include Word-Perfect and Microsoft Word.

Thanks to the World Wide Web, computers around the world are linked together.

A year-end bonus is given to an employee.

year-end bonus

Payment sometimes given to employees at the end of a year in which the employee and/or the company performed very well.

yield

1. The annual **rate of return** on an **investment**, expressed as a percentage.
2. For **bonds** and notes, the coupon rate divided by the **market** price. This is not an accurate measure of total return, since it does not take **capital gains** into consideration.
3. For **securities**, the annual **dividends** divided by the purchase price. This is not an accurate measure of total return, since it does not factor in capital gains.

zero-based budgeting

A management budgeting technique for a **corporation** or government whose goal is to always reexamine the assumptions underlying a company's costs. Zero-based budgeting requires creating a new budget from scratch every year. In order to do so, all spending must be justified each year, not just the amount over of the previous year, which is how typical budgeting is done.

World Wide Web

The total set of **Internet** sites using hypertext transfer protocol (**HTTP**). The hypertext systems provide users with links that connect to other sites anywhere in the world. You must use a web browser, such as Microsoft Explorer or Netscape, to access the World Wide Web.

> "The Internet is an audience of one, a million times over."
> —Peter Gruber, market expert

Are You an Entrepreneur?

So you've answered the questions, and now it's time to find out if you are an entrepreneur. For an in-depth look at your score, check out "What's It All Mean?" for a question-by-question analysis.

1
A) 1 point
B) 5 points
C) 0 points

2
A) 0 points
B) 5 points
C) 1 point

3
A) 1 point
B) 0 points
C) 5 points

4
A) 1 point
B) 0 points
C) 5 points

5
A) 5 points
B) 1 point
C) 0 points

6
A) 0 points
B) 5 points
C) 1 point

7
A) 5 points
B) 1 point
C) 0 points

8
A) 1 point
B) 5 points
C) 0 points

If you answered the questions honestly and scored...

...more than 36 points, congratulations! You already possess many of the qualities necessary to become a successful entrepreneur.

...between 30 and 36 points, you have some of the important traits that support successful entrepreneurship.

...fewer than 30 points, it's possible you may experience some challenges as an entrepreneur—then again, overcoming challenges is what people who build businesses learn how to do.

What's It All Mean?

Here's what the individual answers you gave say about what kind of entrepreneur you might make:

Question One: Entrepreneurs need plenty of "stick-to-it-ive-ness." In this situation, it's easy to think about how much fun watching television and talking with your friend would be. To succeed in starting and running your own business, though, you've got to be ready to take on important work projects (like that report) and not let anything stop you until you complete the work at a high quality level. If you're easily distracted by social events, or likely to do a "rush job" so you can watch something on TV, that's a sign that you may have to change your approach a little when it's time to keep your business up and running.

Question Two: Most successful entrepreneurs are straight shooters. As a rule, they will "lay it all on the line"—even when they know that what they have to say isn't exactly what the other person wants to hear. Of course, many entrepreneurs have a talent for putting the best possible "spin" on the facts, but those who build and grow thriving businesses know that they must be able to stand behind the specific commitments they make to others. The bottom line: If you say what you mean and mean what you say, you will be in a much better position to help sustain your business and maintain your professional relationships.

Question Three: Successful entrepreneurs tend to be self-starters. That means they don't rely on others to get them going or help them set important goals. If you're likely to rely on others to remind you about what you're supposed to be doing—or if you would assign responsibility for failing to walk the dog to someone else-—those aren't good signs for your new business.

Question Four: This one should be pretty obvious. Entrepreneurs often have to make good decisions quickly. If you feel like you need lots of time to make up your mind about something, or you'd rather not make important decisions, then running a company may not be your ideal line of work.

Question Five: Entrepreneurs usually don't have the luxury of stopping when five o'clock rolls around. They have a lot of energy, they may think about work as a kind of play, and they usually see a connection between the rewards they want and their job. If you're uncertain about why you're working on a project, or if you need to be able to "kick back" every night, you may be better off working for someone else.

Question Six: This question is about planning skills. If you want to be successful, you'll have to be able to figure out a step-by-step plan for getting what you want with the resources you've got. Plunging into something without taking possible problems into account can leave you facing big problems. So can waiting for instructions from someone else.

Question Seven: To be a successful entrepreneur, it helps if you can inspire people to do things (like buy from you or work hard on a project) rather than having to convince people to do things. If you'd rather it was someone else's job to get others motivated to take action, you may not be cut out to be an entrepreneur.

Question Eight: While it's true that you did your best, simply saying that to the teacher doesn't say much about your willingness to accept responsibility. Entrepreneurs are leaders who take responsibility for the outcomes of their companies. If you are uncomfortable being accountable to a customer or business ally of your company, you may not be cut out to be an entrepreneur.

HELPFUL RESOURCES

Organizations

Better Business Bureau
www.bbb.org
4200 Wilson Blvd.
Suite 800
Arlington, Virginia 22203-1838
Tel: (703) 276-0100

Business Professionals of America (BPA)
www.bpa.org
5454 Cleveland Ave.
Columbus, Ohio 43231-4021
Tel: (614) 895-7277

Council of Smaller Enterprises (COSE)
www.cose.org
Tower City Center
50 Public Square, Suite 200
Cleveland, Ohio 44113-2291
Tel: (888) 304-GROW

Education, Training and Enterprise Center (EDTEC)
www.edtecinc.com
313 Market Street
Camden, New Jersey 08102
Tel: (800) 963-9361

Federation of Tax Administrators
www.taxadmin.org
444 N. Capital St., NW, Suite 348
Washington, DC 20001
Tel: (202) 624-5890

International Trademark Association (INTA)
www.inta.org
1133 Avenue of the Americas
New York, New York 10036
Tel: (212) 768-9887

National Coalition for Empowering Youth Entrepreneurs, Inc. (NCEYE)
www.agnr.umd.edu/users/kidbiz/
nceyehist.html
3597 Shannon Drive
Baltimore, Maryland 21213

National Education Center for Women in Business
maura.setonhill.edu/~necwb/
Seton Hill College
Seton Hill Drive
Greensburg, Pennsylvania 15601
Tel: (800) 826-6234

National Federation of Community Development Credit Unions
www.natfed.org
120 Wall Street, 10th Floor
New York, New York 10005
Tel: (212) 809-1850

National Foundation for Teaching Entrepreneurship
www.nfte.com
120 Wall Street, 29th Floor
New York, New York 10005
Tel: (212) 232-3333

Rural Entrepreneurship Through Action Learning (REAL)
www.realenterprises.org
115 Market Street, Suite 320
Durham, North Carolina 27701
Tel: (919) 688-7325

Service Corp of Retired Executives (SCORE)
www.score.org
409 3rd Street, SW, 6th Floor
Washington, DC 20024
Tel: (800) 634-0245

Women's Business Enterprise National Council
www.wbenc.org
1120 Connecticut Ave., NW
Suite 950
Washington, DC 20036
Tel: (202) 872-5515

Young Americans Bank and Education Foundation
www.theyoungamericans.org
311 Steele Street
Denver, Colorado 80206
Tel: (303) 321-2265

YoungBiz.com
www.youngbiz.com
5589 Peachtree Rd.
Chamblee, Georgia 30341
Tel: (888) KIDSWAY

Youth Venture
www.youthventure.org
1700 North Moore Street
Suite 1920
Arlington, Virginia 22209
Tel: (703) 527-8300

Government Organizations

Business Information Centers (BICs)
www.sba.gov/bi/bics/
A division of the U.S. Small Business Administration that provides reference libraries of books, publications, videos, and online resources for business assistance.

Consumer Information Center
www.pueblo.gsa.gov
P.O. Box 100
Pueblo, Colorado 81002
Tel: (719) 948-4000

Internal Revenue Service
www.irs.gov
P.O. Box 25866
Richmond, Virginia 23260
Tel: (800) 424-3676

Occupational Safety & Health Administration
www.osha.gov
200 Constitution Avenue, NW
Washington, DC 20210
Tel: (800) 321-OSHA

U.S. Chamber of Commerce
www.uschamber.com
1615 H Street, NW
Washington, DC 20062
Tel: (202) 659-6000

U.S. Consumer Product Safety Commission

www.cpsc.gov
Publications Request
Washington, DC 20207
Tel: (800) 638-2772

U.S. Copyright Office

www.loc.gov/copyright/
Library of Congress
101 Independence Avenue, SE
Washington, DC 20559
Tel: (202) 707-3000

U.S. Equal Employment Opportunity Commission

www.eeoc.gov
1801 L Street, NW
Washington, DC 20507
Tel: (800) 669-4000

U.S. Patent & Trademark Office (USPTO)

www.uspto.gov
General Information Services
Division
Crystal Plaza 3, Room 2C02
Washington, DC 20231
Tel: (800) 786-9199

U.S. Small Business Administration (SBA)

www.sba.gov
409 3rd Street, SW
Washington, DC 20416
Tel: (800) 827-5722

Web Sites

www.allbusiness.com
Resources for market research, public relations, and customer service

www.bizplanit.com
An Internet-based business plan consulting firm whose Web site includes lots of free information.

www.craftsreport.com
An e-zine covering the crafts industry, includes business resources for craftspeople

www.entreworld.org
Features helpful advice and articles on starting your own business or expanding the business you already have.

www.ltbn.com
Resource for entrepreneurs, including articles and interviews with small business people.

www.npr.org
The National Public Radio site has information about entrepreneurship and small business management.

www.onlinebusadv.com
Free information and advice on business and management, including customer service, hiring policies, and strategic planning.

www.sba.gov/sbdc
This Web site offers management assistance to current and prospective business owners.

www.sbaer.uca.edu
An electronic resource information center that offers some of the newest and most current information on advances in small business technology.

www.sbaonline.sba.gov
The U.S. Small Business Administration has an excellent Web site specifically focused on government resources for small businesses; it has articles and extensive links around the Web.

www.yeo.org
The Young Entrepreneurs Organization (YEO) is a nonprofit, educational organization dedicated to assisting young entrepreneurs.

Books

50 Moneymaking Ideas for Kids by Lauree Burkett and L. Allen. Thomas Nelson: Nashville, TN, 1997.

Better Than A Lemonade Stand by Daryl Bernstein. Beyond Words Publishings: Hillsboro, OR, 1992.

The New Youth Entrepreneur by Marilyn Kourilsky, Carol Allen, Aaron Bocage, and George Waters. EDTEC and the Kauffman Center for Entrepreneurial Leadership: Kansas City, MO, 1995.

Totally Awesome Business Book For Kids by Adrian Berg and Arthur Berg Bochner. Newmarket Press. New York, 1995.

Venture Adventure by Daryl Bernstein. Beyond Words Publishing: Hillsboro, OR, 1996.

Young Entrepreneurs Guide to Starting and Running a Business by Steve Mariotti with Debra DeSalvo and Tony Towle. Times Books, a division of Random House: New York, 1996.

BIBLIOGRAPHY

Books

Albrecht, Donna G. *Promoting Your Business with Free (or Almost Free) Publicity* (Run Your Own Business). Englewood Cliffs, NJ: Prentice Hall Trade, 1997.

Elias, Stephan and Kate McGrath. *Trademark: Legal Care for Your Business and Product Name,* Fourth Edition. Berkeley, CA: Nolo Press, 1999.

Fishman, Stephen. *The Copyright Handbook—How to Protect and Use Written Works,* Fourth Edition. Berkeley, CA: Nolo Press, 1998.

Green, Charles H. *The SBA Loan Book.* Avon, MA: Adams Media Corporation, 1999.

Klein, Erica Levy. *Write Great Ads: A Step-by-Step Approach.* New York: John Wiley & Sons, 1990.

Lonier, Terri. *Working Slob,* Second Edition. New York: John Wiley & Sons, 1998.

Peterson, Mark A. *The Complete Entrepreneur: The Only Book You'll Ever Need to Manage Risk and Build Your Business Wealth.* Hauppauge, NY: Barron's Educational Series, 1996.

Pinson, Linda and Jerry Jinnett. *Anatomy of a Business Plan,* Third Edition. Chicago: Upstart Publishing Company, 1996.

Schiffman, Stephan. *The Consultant's Handbook: How to Start and Develop Your Own Practice,* Second Edition. Avon, MA: Adams Media Corporation, 2000.

Schiffman, Stephan. *Make It Your Business: The Definitive Guide to Starting and Succeeding in Your Own Business.* New York: Pocket Book, 1998.

Schlit, W. Keith. *The Entrepreneurs Guide to Preparing a Winning Business Plan and Raising Venture Capital.* New York: Simon & Schuster, 1990.

Timm, Paul R. *50 Powerful Ways to Win New Customers: Fast, Simple, Inexpensive, Profitable and Proven Ideas You Can Use Starting Today!* Franklin Lakes, NJ: Career Press, 1997.

White, Sarah and John Woods. *Do-It-Yourself Advertising.* Avon, MA: Adams Media Corporation, 1997.

Web Sites

D.E.I. Management Group
www.dei-sales.com
Learn about effective selling strategies in phone prospecting, selling skills, prospect management, and much more.

Small Business Development Center
http://sbdcnet.utsa.edu/
A huge array of research and planning tools for the small business community; also offers a wealth of helpful articles, templates, and statistical overviews.

U.S. Small Business Administration (SBA)
www.sba.gov
Information on how the SBA can help you start, finance and expand a business, including links to many federal, state and local government web sites.

Young Entprepreneur
www.youngentrepreneur.com
Comprehensive on-line resource for young entrepreneurs and growing businesses.

Young Entrepreneur's Organization
www.yeo.org
A global, non-profit educational organization for business owners under age 40.

marketing, **62**, 65
  demographics, 36
  direct mail, 37, 61
  e-mail, 100
  loss leader, 60
  multi-level (MLM), 68
  niche, 72
  promotion, 81
  psychographics, 82
  telemarketing, 103
  See also advertising
marketing materials, **65**
marketing mix, **65**, 80
marketing research, **65**
mentor, **65–66**
merchandise, 57, 63, **66**, 68
merchant account, **66**
merchant bank, **67**
merger, 46, **67**, 69
mission statement, **67**
monopoly, **69**
mortgage, 26, **67–68**, 71
  foreclosure, 46
multi-level-marketing (MLM), **68**
multinational, **68**, 88
municipal bonds, 19
mutual fund, **68**

NASDAQ (National Association of Securities Dealers), 70
negotiation, **70**
net, 63, **70**
net worth, **71**
networking, **70–71**
New York Stock Exchange, 42, **71**, 115
newsgroup, **71**
newsletter, **72**
  online, 74
niche, **72**, 88
niche marketing, **72**
not-for-profit organization, **72**
note, **72**
  short-term, 99
notice, **72**

online, **74**
online newsletter, **74**
online service, 66, **74**
operating cost, **74**, 81
option, 71, **74**
outsourcing, **75**
overhead, 70, 74, **75**, 101

paper loss, **76**
paper profit, **76**
partnership, **78**
  joint venture, 57
  silent partner, 99
patent, 52, **76**
pay-per-click, **76–77**
payables, **76**
pension, **77**
pension plan, **77**
  SEP-IRA, 95–96
  simple IRA, 99
  vesting, 113
performance appraisal, **77**
point of sale (POS), **77**
portfolio, **79**
positioning, 62, **79**
power of attorney, 79
preemptive right, **79**
preferred stock, 71, **79–80**
press release, **80**
price, 54, 55, 57, 65, 69, 74, 75, **80–81**, 93
  Consumer Price Index, 16, 31
  cost per thousand, 34
  fair market value, 43
  market value, 64
  promotional, 81
price ceiling, **81**
price floor, **81**
product line, **81**, 100
profit and loss (P&L) statement, **81**
programmer, **81**
promotion, 62, 65, **81**, 86
promotional pricing, **81**
prospecting, **82**
prototype, **82**
psychographics, **82**
public domain, **82**
public relations, 62, 80, **82**
publicity, **82**

quality control, **84**
quarterly report, **84**
quick ratio, **84**
quick turn, **85**
quota, **85**

rate, **85**
rate of exchange, **85**
rate of return, **85**

raw materials, **85**
real estate, 26, 39, **86**, 104
rebate, **86**
receipt, **86**
receivables, **86**
recession, 22, **86**
redeemable, **87**
refinancing, **87**
refund, **87**
rent, 16, 72, 74, 75, **87**
replacement cost, **87**
reserve, **89**
reserve requirements, **88**
residuals, **89**
retail, 57, 60, 62, 81, **88**
  chain store, 25
  loss leader, 60
  merchandise, 66
  merchant account, 66
retailer, 57, **89**
  specialty, 100
retirement, 77, **89**
return on equity (ROE), **90**
return on investment, (ROI), **90**
revenue, 81, **90**, 101, 104
revolving credit agreement, **90**
revolving line of credit, **90**
risk, 87, **90**
router, **90**
royalty, **90**

S corporation, 51, **91**
salary, **91**
sales, **91**
  call center, 23
  cold call, 27
  discount, 37
  e-commerce, 40
  market share, **64**
  revenue, 90
  upselling, 109
  See also marketing; retail
sales force, **92**
sales forecast, **92**
sales management, **92**
sales representative, **92**
sales tax, **93**
sample, **93**
saturation, **93**
savings account, **93**
savings and loan, **93**
scarcity, **93**
search engine, **93**
search engine placement, **93**
secondary market, **95**